WHEN YOU SOW YOU DON'T REAP

BEING PATIENT IN AN IMPATIENT WORLD

RUDOLPH MENSAH

COPYRIGHT © 2020, RUDOLPH MENSAH

The stories I share in this book are true life events of my childhood. I have recollected and told them in a way to enhance and establish the subject this book deals with; learning to be patient. My mum and siblings are in on this-. Any other stories I share which involve other people, I have protected their identity by merely referring to their gender instead of names or other personal identities linking them to the stories.

Reviewers may quote brief passages in reviews.

FOR COPIES OF THIS BOOK / TO BOOK FOR SPEAKING ENGAGEMENTS, KINDLY CONTACT THE AUTHOR VIA:
E-mail: rudolphmensah87@gmail.com

Phone: +233-247-930389/+233-592932624
Facebook: Rudolph Mensah
Instagram/Twitter: @MensahRudolph
Author: www.amazon.com/author/rudolphmensah

DEDICATION

To every millennial out there feeling like their life is a mess and everyone else is ahead of them.

Maybe they are actually ahead depending on the unit of measurement you are using to measure your progress or perhaps it's not that they are ahead but you are probably comparing your seed with their harvest.

To my mum for taking me to the farm and exposing me to the realities of life on the farm.

"*patience is becoming a rare commodity in our generation; everyone wants it yesterday.*"

Rudolph Mensah

Contents

FOREWORD

Life is lived in stages, seasons and times. The strength, depth, and reach of a life is dependent on the ability to maximize each season to its fullest capacity. Often, many live for the season of harvest, the time of fruits, progress, and results yet very few are willing to fully give themselves to the season of painful tilling, sowing, watering, nursing to yield a healthy bumper harvest.

Many entrepreneurs, celebrities, ministers experience short term success not given themselves to the training that will propel their longevity in their arena of operation, they sprout out of a short season and wither away shortly.

Rudolph Mensah captures and meticulously discusses the importance and the need for patience in achieving greatness and lasting success.

To a generation who's lost the art of waiting and the beauty of endurance in achieving a lasting legacy, this book, **WHEN YOU SOW YOU DON'T REAP IMMEDIATELY,** serves as a needed reminder to emulate the patience of the Lord Jesus, who took 30 years to prepare for a 3 year ministry.

We often attribute the success of Jesus's ministry to His divinity forgetting that while on earth, he fully functioned as a man. In the 30 years, Jesus "sowed" himself to patient, training and preparation, and was rewarded in Luke 2:52.

And Jesus increased in wisdom and stature, and in favour with God and men, Luke 2:52.

Rudolph captures the principles that birth the success of Luke 2:52. He encourages His readers to be diligent, hardworking, protect their seed, identify the internal and external threats to their success, and when all due diligence is done, have the courage to wait for the manifestation of which you planted.

A masterpiece from an articulate and coherent writer. I recommend this book to everyone who is seeking to achieve notable and lasting success. The wisdom in this book will be a needed resource for your journey. Well Done Rudolph, Thank you.

... See how the farmer waits for the precious fruit of the earth, waiting patiently for it until it receives the early and latter rain. James 5:7

Graciously contributed by Dr Alex Opoku, Associate Professor at the University College London (UCL) and Cost Management Consultant with expertise in sustainable built environment

PROLOGUE: WHEN YOU SOW, YOU WAIT BEFORE YOU REAP

Growing up, I spent time on the farm. I detested every minute of it. Don't call me names, I was 10. Name as many ten-year-old boys in the world who went to farm almost every day of the week, had a full day's work and occasionally had to go fetch firewood on Sundays before going to church. I bet that would be a pretty small list.

Just before you get any ideas, this was a period of my life growing up when my family experienced the bitter bile of life. Right up until then, we enjoyed the sweetness of life. I am grateful for the balance; it helps me to appreciate life.

Reminiscing, this was a time which taught me a lot of lessons. I learnt valuable lessons about commitment, hard work, discipline, faith and trusting in the process. On the farm, I learnt that you don't reap immediately after you sow.

In our current day and age, we are caught up with the phrase; "you reap what you sow" so much that we think the next thing right after you sow is to reap.

We miss the process completely. We skip waiting for rain or irrigation, germination, weeding, waiting, applying fertilizers if need be, weeding again, waiting some more, more rain or if the rains delay, we irrigate, pruning, waiting for plants to bear fruits or crops, waiting for it to mature, waiting to harvest, harvesting, drying, storing. This is quite a long process, but we are a generation looking to reap right after we sow. Nature, however, is orderly. We can never go against nature. You can't skip steps in life. You can try to but life will bring you back to the step you missed. You have to learn all your lessons before you can move on. Life will keep you repeating a phase until you learn your lesson.

The earlier you put yourself through the process, the better for you. You must accept that life is a process. You can facilitate the process; you can reduce the learning curve by learning from others who have gone ahead but you can never skip steps.

There is a lot of hard work from sowing to reaping. In our era where everyone is going nowhere fast, patience is becoming a rare commodity especially among the youth. In this book, I am looking to share these valuable lessons I learnt on the farm with you. The need to trust the process and believe that when we put in the work, the results will come, as Michael Jordan once opined.

It is difficult to wait; it takes a lot of energy to wait for success. No kidding, it takes a lot of tenacity to wait when everyone else seems to be moving forward. It requires fortitude to be patient when others seem to be ahead of you. It takes patience to withhold from striking when the opportunity presents itself. It takes patience to not spend when you have the money. To trust the process and not rush, understanding that great things require patience. The weak cannot wait. Only the strong can wait. Those who have the tenacity to wait enjoy long term success. The weak fret and give up. They take the easy options. They concentrate on the now. They grasp for short term gratification losing sight of the long-term satisfaction and true fulfillment.

Nothing happens overnight and so without patience, many give up. We settle for the seemingly short-term victories. Remember, what you seek won't happen overnight. You won't build a lasting relationship overnight, you won't make an impact in your career overnight, and you won't become a millionaire overnight. You won't become successful overnight. You won't become a bestseller because you wrote one book.

No one starts from the top. The only time you start from the top is when you are digging a grave. You have to be patient and willing to start from the bottom. Build your way up. Put in the work; believe we shall win, maybe not immediately but definitely.

Young people have fallen into "Ponzi schemes" promising instant success. People join network marketing companies looking to make big success overnight. For clarity sake, I am not equating "Ponzi schemes" to "multilevel network marketing".

Quickly, please don't close the book if you are an associate of a network marketing company; don't get me wrong, it takes hard work, discipline and commitment to succeed in the business.

My concern here is with the unrealistic promises some companies make to their associates. Also, many associates have an erroneous idea or perception of what it will take to succeed. They see the cars and money and they believe just by joining they will make it overnight. We would both agree that it takes a lot of grit, patience and commitment to make it to the top.

It takes patience, dedication and commitment to build anything worthwhile and this includes network marketing. It requires persistence to succeed.

Patience is the subject of this book and my main goal is to let you fully understand that it will take time to succeed at anything. Don't be influenced by the cars and money they show you or you see.

Nothing happens overnight, unless you rob a bank. If you are looking to rob a bank, I can't help you. You can stop reading this book now. It has nothing to offer you with your quest.

In this book we are going to learn how to make it, trusting in the process and enjoying the journey. I have come to the conclusion that overnight success usually takes about ten (10) to fifteen (15) years.

The "successful people" you see have been working without recognition for at least ten (10) years. It is my hope that young people of the 21st century will learn and master the art of patience using this book as a guide.

The germination process was mind blowing to me at a young age. How it sprouted out of the dark loamy earth blossoming into green plants.

I need you to understand this point; an effort without immediate result is painful and that is why many give up. We want everything quickly; patience is therefore becoming a rare commodity.

This is a generation which is losing the art of waiting for results I have a life philosophy that I am known for and I want you to imbibe it; "WE SHALL WIN, MAYBE NOT IMMEDIATELY BUT DEFINITELY".

I trust the process. I believe in the process. To clarify something significant before we dive in, there is a clear difference between waiting and laziness. You don't laze about and say you are waiting. Whilst our maize plant was growing, we weeded and sometimes applied manure. We worked our field. We didn't just sit around waiting for the maize to mature on its own.

So, I am not talking about being lazy as being patient. Whatever dream you are working on, if you have sowed, understand that you have to wait. You have to build yourself. It won't happen overnight. We shall win, maybe not immediately but definitely.

Rudolph Mensah

Author, Doctor (MH) and Motivational Doer

"Listen carefully: Unless a grain of wheat is buried in the ground, dead to the world, it is never any more than a grain of wheat. But if it is buried, it sprouts and reproduces itself many times over."

John 12:24 MSG

CHAPTER ONE: THE SEED (IDEA)

"The soil says, don't bring me your need, bring me your seed." - Jim Rohn

EVERYONE has an idea. Everyone has a seed. Some succeed with their idea, many don't. Some gather into barns during harvest, others beg in harvest. What makes the difference? Execution! Many seeds are not planted. Seeds not planted die. The same way, many ideas are not executed. Ideas are easy to come by, comparatively, implementation is hard. The farmers who reap bountiful harvest are the ones who plant their seeds, work around them and have the patience to wait for the harvest.

Some farmers plant their seeds, and then leave them to be choked by weeds, to rot. Other farmers plant their seeds, work around them for a while and then get tired. They leave them to wither in the sun. The neglected plants yield poor harvest and are often eaten by rodents.

There is another group of farmers. They do everything right but then when the maize starts bearing crops, they don't have the patience to wait for it to mature. They harvest prematurely.

I was part of the last group growing up. It's a lot of hard

work from planting to reaping. It wasn't only for me as a ten-year old but also for everyone involved in farming.

The first principle I learnt on the maize farm was that, "you must first plant your seed, which is the first qualification you have for a harvest." Having seeds means nothing until you plant them. Growing up, there were some people in our village who would rather go hungry or steal than to till their own land.

It was hard work. You had to do it hungrily, you had to sacrifice and not everyone is ready for that. Without planting your seeds, you have automatically disqualified yourself from reaping.

The second principle I learnt on the maize farm was, "you either work your field during the planting season or beg for food during the harvest."

Planting your seed is only the first step. An important step as it is, it's not the end because many seeds die after planting. The real work begins after planting.

The work involved after planting requires total commitment and effort many are not willing to invest. Just having an idea is not enough to succeed. You must be willing to put in the work. Many give up or complain about how hard it is to grow the seeds. If anyone told you it would be easy, they lied. It was never easy on the farm.

Just like planting your seed is an important step in having a harvest, starting is an important step for your idea but it takes tenacity to see it through.

In this chapter, I am likening our ideas to seeds so we can understand why so many ideas never see the light of day. So, we can learn how to plant our ideas and grow them to fruition. As Earl Nightengale said, "Everything begins with an idea."

The seed is a valuable determinant in the kind of harvest we reap. Without a seed, there is nothing to sow, nothing to germinate, nothing to grow and nothing to harvest.

In the same vein, without an idea, you have nothing to work on, nothing to develop and nothing to succeed with. The idea is therefore the most important factor in beginning the pursuit of purpose just as the seed is.

One principle my mum taught me growing up on the farm; she said "the maize seed is the most important item in our house. Whether we had maize seeds or otherwise, the planting season would determine whether we will have food to eat or beg food in harvest."

Even if we had no money but seeds, we were assured of a harvest if we worked hard on the farm. That has been the foundation of my life, all I need to move myself forward is an idea. It forces you to be resourceful instead of giving up on life because of the lack of resources.

The Akan ethnic group in Ghana has interesting meanings of the names for the months of the year. I am a Fante, a Tribe in the Akan ethnic group and I will explain to you how we call the months of the year.

I will explain that of June, July and August for emphasis on why farming taught me a lot in life.

The month of June, in the Fante language, is known as "Obiredzi", literally meaning "suffer to eat". The month of March and April are mostly the time when we prepare our lands for the planting season awaiting the rain. The month of May is when the rains are expected to start falling.

Most of the agricultural activities in Ghana are dependent on natural rainfall. When nature denied us rain, we were denied our harvest.

The month of June, is a time for waiting. In this month, we had planted our maize, weeded around it; hopefully the rains keep coming down as needed. At this point, the maize plants are green on the farm and some may have started flowering. It depends on how early we sowed our seeds. Some hybrid maize seeds mature in 3 months, our local maize seeds will usually take about 6 months to mature.

In the month of June, when we have planted our maize seeds, there is no food to eat. Most of our staple foods came from maize and cassava flour. This means we must "suffer to eat". This is why the Fantes call the month of June "Obiredzi".

In the month of June, we have spent all our money and every resource we have on keeping the farm healthy. Weeding and making sure rodents don't destroy our maize plants. We buy pesticides if needed, we hire labourers to weed if the farm is too big for the nuclear family to work on, so; we "suffer to eat." This is the month of endurance; our hope is in our harvest. We have sacrificed everything believing we will reap.

Next is the month of July known as "Ayewoho". This means

"you have regretted". Why the regret?

During the planting season, not every member of the community is engaged in farming activities. I grew up in a community with two primary occupations, fishing and farming. Some people engaged in neither occupation.

For this group of neither farmers nor fishers, July is a month of reckoning and regrets. July is the time when the maize plants begin to bear crops and mature.

This is a time of regret for this group of people who neither farmed nor fished.

As people are getting ready to harvest their produce from the farm, they have nothing to look forward to.

That is why we call the month of July, "month of regret" for those who were idle during the planting season.

Sounds interesting, right?

Lastly, the month of August is known as "Dzifuu". This means "you have plenty to eat" or "eat to the full". This is the time when farmers harvest their farm produce and fishers have the bumper harvest of fish. Therefore, those who planted, worked on their farm and waited through the dry periods of June and July now have a cause to celebrate. They can eat and enjoy the fruits of their labour, even in excess. Food to eat, fish to eat!

This is why my mum, regardless of how hard things were in March, April, May, June and July, always looked forward to August. She doesn't want to regret in "ayewoho" because she knows "Dzifuu" is coming.

The temptation to eat your seeds and not plant was there every planting season. Was I ever tempted to roast the maize seeds? Yes, a lot of times! There was this time that I roasted maize seeds meant for planting. I think I was about 11.

I have a scar to show for it. My mum always protected her seeds.

We have already established the principle expounded in this book that the seed is like an idea.

"All achievements, all earned riches, have their beginning in an idea."- Napoleon Hill.

Like my mum, what length will you go to protect your seeds? Some of us are careless with our ideas just as some are careless with their seeds.

"The seeds are for planting not eating."-
Helena Inkoom (Mum)

How often do people eat their seeds? A lot! How often do we discard our ideas? A lot! It is strange to know that the seed however was one of the most neglected things on the farm. People drop them by the farm path. We saw several maize seeds on the way by the time we arrived on our farm, a distance of about 7-10 miles from home. Along the path, I would find and count tens of seeds dropped by the farmers on their way to the farm.

I believe every idea is like a seed. How you treat it determines your harvest.

Everyone has ideas. Ideas don't discriminate. Anyone can

14

generate ideas if he or she is willing to commit to thinking and looking out for solutions to problems we find around us.

Ideas are natural; ideas don't care whether you are black or white, tall or short, rich or poor. Anyone can generate ideas.

So are seeds. Seeds don't care who owns them. Anyone can own the seed. What you do with it, however, determines what kind of harvest you get. You can eat your seeds, you can ignore them; you can throw them away and hope they germinate or you can nurture them.

Next, the size of the seed doesn't matter or determine the size of the harvest. That I also learnt on the farm. I always wondered, as a ten-year old, how can a small maize seed produce these numbers of maize crops? A small maize seed when planted, watered, nurtured, weeded around, can produce maize crops with hundreds of maize seeds. The size didn't matter. You just have to plant it and work around it.

"Ideas can be life-changing. Sometimes all you need to open the door is just one more good idea." --- Jim Rohn

A single idea may be all that you will need to succeed. The size of the idea doesn't matter; you just have to get to work on it. You don't need to start a company like Microsoft or Apple to become successful, you don't need to be another Jack Ma, all you need is a single idea you are willing to dedicate and commit your time to. It will give you a harvest beyond your expectation.

GROWING THE SEEDS

How do seeds grow?

I have given a lot of thoughts to what happened on the farm. With my growing knowledge in Science and experience over the years, it is now clear to me what went on from the time of planting to the time of reaping. I will be sharing that with you in this book as promised.

What I want you to take away from this book is to find out how you can grow that idea of yours just as we grow seeds.

Seeds require certain factors to survive. These may be environmental or the genetic composition of the seed itself.

There are certain conditions necessary for the survival of a seed; water, sunlight, humidity, protection from insects, etc. These are some of the factors needed for a seed to thrive and finally germinate.

It was our responsibility to ensure our maize seeds were safe and healthy till we planted them. Only healthy seeds germinated and produced healthy crops. If you want a good harvest, take care of your seeds. I learnt that early on the farm.

And just like a seed, every idea needs certain factors to survive, and not die. This is important because it is easy to get an idea (at least a lot of people get ideas everyday) but not so many ideas survive. There are many distractions and harsh realities out there. Many ideas don't live on to fruition.

On one of the episodes on my BECOMING YOUR DREAM podcast, I had an interview on the subject, WHAT TO DO WITH IDEAS. Find link in the introductory pages and listen to that particular episode. Everyone has an idea, everyone has talent [even those who say they don't] but you should know that…

"Talent is cheaper than table salt. What separates the talented individual from the successful one is a lot of hard work." - Stephen King

It's not just talent which requires hard work to thrive but that's what ideas need to become successful. Hard work is the difference between successful ideas and unsuccessful ones.

I am going to take you through the process of germination and highlight the factors necessary for a seed to stay viable for germination to occur.

We will then translate this to how we can keep our ideas viable and grow them. I believe if we can understand how seeds survive and germinate, we can apply these principles and processes to our ideas and make them thrive.

What is a seed?

A seed is a matured fertilized plant ovule consisting of an embryo and its food source and having a protective coat or testa.

A seed after being fully matured first has to be kept in the right environment.

THE RIGHT ENVIRONMENT

What factors constitute the right environment?

The right environment for the seed here is somehow a broad description which includes the right amount of sunlight, avoiding extreme humidity and avoiding pests and insects eating them. The seed can only survive when these factors are well within normal.

Ideas also need the right environment. Ideas need sunlight.

Moisture is also a factor which may affect the viability of seeds. Too much moisture may rot a seed. Ideas when exposed to moisture may also rot.

Don't allow people to spit negativity on your ideas. That's moisture. There are people who think every idea is wrong. They will never support any idea you have, sometimes, just because it's coming from you. You remember when you wanted to sell ice cream and they scorned you off?

And when you told them you wanted to start selling shoes and they laughed that off as well? How about when you wanted to audition for that movie and they said you were not good enough?

Why do you keep telling them your ideas? So, they can keep spitting on them?

Stay away from negative people, someone once said "they have a problem for every solution". Never get entangled with people who are always looking at the negative side of your idea. They can give you a hundred and one (101) reasons why it won't work instead of finding one (1) reason why it would. Look for people who will say, "Great idea but this won't work because of this and that, how about doing it this way to see if that will work? Have you tried it this way?"

Surround yourself with people who are solution minded, not magnifiers of problems. Everyone can point out what's wrong. Very few people can provide solutions to what's wrong. Those who succeed are those who are always looking out for solutions.

I believe that no one knows enough to be a pessimist but you will have a lot of people doubting you. Don't doubt yourself. You have to protect your idea from negativity, doubt and pessimism.

Let me quickly dispel a notion you may be getting from the paragraphs above. I am not saying every idea you will have would be great. Don't think of anyone who would question your idea to be spitting on it. No, no, if that's how you understood me, I am so sorry for "supposedly" misleading you. Let me re-route and bring you to my point. I am not telling you to see everyone who opposes your idea as the enemy, no, never. Your enemy would be happy to see you fail with your bad idea. They will tell you it's a great idea when in fact it's bad.

The one who is only criticizing your idea without offering you solutions or how to make it better is spitting on your idea. That is not good moisture for your seed. The one who is pointing out how weak your idea is, or asking questions while offering alternatives or solutions is actually helping your idea to survive the environment out there.

In order for your idea to succeed, you need someone to look you in the eyes and tell you your idea isn't going to survive out there. You need someone to tell you what's wrong with your idea. You need someone who can tell you that your idea isn't going to work, and you need to rethink it.

Finally, you will need someone to tell you that the great idea you think you are the only genius to come up with is actually a porous one in need of mending. The person who stands up to you; questions your idea, letting you know all the possible obstacles you haven't imagined is your friend. If this person then goes on to tell you how to prepare your idea for it to survive out there, you should appreciate it more than anything in your life. Listen to that person. He or she loves you more than anyone.

That has been the role of my mentor. The moment I get any idea, I just throw it to him. At the first sniff of it, I know he has questions lined up for me. I am expectant of getting lots of questions about my idea. He knows how to ask the right questions. That's the right environment for your idea to succeed. When I had the idea to write one of my books, I told him on Whatsapp. He asked all the right questions.

He read a part of the first draft and said to me: "I feel like you haven't done your best on this one. Take some time and work on it then maybe I can spend some more time on it."

It was hard to take at first. I had a feeling he should at least read it all. But after I evaluated his comments and what I had done, I knew that wasn't anywhere near my best. I went back to work on it. Before we planted our seeds on the farm, there was an important process called "winnowing" we undertook. This was a process whereby seeds are examined and inspected physically to take out the dead or bad ones leaving only the healthy ones. It was a lot of work but mum would make us do it prior to planting, every time.

Whether beans or maize seeds, we would carefully collect the dead or bad seeds and throw them away leaving only the healthy seeds. Winnowing is such an important process and we need to do the same thing for our ideas.

In order to be left with healthy ideas, we need to take our ideas through winnowing. It was hard to take out some of our seeds and throw them away. They were all our seeds. We loved our seeds but when it came to winnowing, all dead seeds were thrown out. Only healthy seeds got planted.

However nice your ideas may sound; you need to pass them through winnowing.

We are often biased with our own ideas. We cherish them. Protect them. Our idea is our baby. You don't want to hurt it. You don't want to throw it out. You don't want people to tell you how bad your idea is.

It sounds great to you until you expose it to the world. You only begin to realize the deficiencies in your idea when you winnow it.

In order not to risk losing it altogether, be courageous enough to take your ideas through winnowing. Often, with a trusted mentor like I do with mine. Someone who will carefully examine your ideas and let you know what's dead.

You can't however take your idea through winnowing with just anyone. You have to avoid the chronic pessimist who provides no solutions but condemns every idea you present to him or her. My mentor will say, "I think you haven't given a thorough thought to your idea. Go and search some more, look deeper, what you have is good but I don't see how it is going to work in the real world. Have you considered what will happen if this or that should happen? How are you going to generate revenue with that? Unless you want to run a charity, take some time and look at it again."

This is not him being negative or spitting on my idea. That is him giving me a reality check. We all need that for our ideas to survive. We don't pamper ideas; we bring it out in the open to be scrutinized. Take them through winnowing.

Just as seeds need sunlight, it's also important for us to expose our ideas to sunlight. Every idea needs sunlight. Never keep it in your head thinking you have found something wonderful, something no one has ever thought about. Sorry, King Solomon of the ancient Israel kingdom said something in the book of Ecclesiastes; "there is nothing new under the sun" and I agree with him.

Every idea you have, either someone is doing something similar out there or doing the exact thing, perhaps, in another way. Bring your idea out into the light, expose it to the sunlight and learn. Ask questions, be asked questions, and expose your idea to sunlight.

It's important to remember, an overexposure to sunlight can destroy a seed. The right amount of sunlight is needed for the seed to stay viable.

Exposing our ideas to people is a risk many are afraid to take. The most important thing is to expose it to the right people. There are people who can't stand our ideas, some might chastise you, despise you and say negative things. There are others who will offer nothing, there are those who may steal it, there are others who will shoot it down; there are a few others who would simply be indifferent.

The question then is; how do we expose our idea to the right amount of sunlight? How do we find the right people to talk to? Most important question again is; "who is the right person?"

Someone you work with, someone you trust, a partner, family member, a mentor, etc. Talk to mentors, talk to leaders you trust, friends you can confide in, expose your idea to sunlight. Let them criticize it, let them offer ideas, let them shine some more light on it so your idea can survive.

I know, please relax, you are still asking, how do I know who is the right person to expose my idea to? Alright, I am not going to run away from your question; I am going to tell you one way I do it and maybe you can adopt that and modify it for yourself.

First, it is always important to find someone who has already done it or in the process of doing it. You don't want to share your idea about starting an online business with someone who has no idea about what it takes to build an online business.

Talk to people who bring experience to the table. You can

talk to people who may not have industry experience in what you want to do but they can offer you experience they have from doing other businesses in other industries. The point is, don't talk to someone about starting a business, who never started a business himself/herself. Everything he or she tells you would be theory and no practical experience.

What most people are worried about is trust, you will need to trust some people with your ideas. There is a study which said that the most successful people in life are those who share their thoughts and ideas. As my friend Samuel Abeiku Dadson says, "no one has monopoly on an idea". When you share your ideas, those who have already done it or have learnt from the process of doing something similar will share with you the specifics that enabled them to get to where they are or where they got to. This will help you map out the best plan for your own ideas.

When you share your ideas with people who have already done it, there is no doubt that you will think and reason better on your idea than you were initially. You will gain clarity about what you want to do. On conceiving the idea for my first book, BECOMING YOUR DREAM, which was initially thought of for a small group of students I needed to write for, I had to share the idea with my friend and partner, Solomon Ewusie. We talked about having a book like that which will help young people find their paths in life and become what they dream of. I also shared the idea with my mentor and then with one other friend. After talking to 3-5 people about it, I had a deeper understanding of what I wanted to do.

The lesson here is, before you plant your seed, expose it to sunlight. Before you implement any idea, talk to someone. Discuss it; let them ask you questions, something my mentor is great at. Anytime I want to challenge my ideas, I will share it with him. He has a way of asking the right questions to get you thinking deeper in ways you never imagined. We need these people to help our ideas grow. In your head, it may sound all special. It would look like the best idea you have ever had but if you share it with others, you get the opportunity to receive honest feedback.

What most people are afraid of is actually who to talk to, right? Yeah, I know how you feel about that. I haven't forgotten your question. Now, here is my answer:

There are different kinds of people we will encounter the moment we set out to share our ideas. Obviously, there are many who will be willing to assist us, help us out just as equally as there are others who will have nothing good to offer.

Not only that, they may be negative influence on our ideas. Some people make it their personal ambition to always discourage you on your ideas.

Who do you talk to?

Talk to the optimistic and highly motivated people. These are the ones who will keep you positive about everything you do.

This doesn't mean they would pamper you or wouldn't tell you where you are wrong. They would tell you what you should do differently, they will tell you what you need to know and share with you what you need to do to make the idea work.

I have a way of talking to people about my ideas. I first speak to people about my ideas in very few sentences; I pause, and watch the demeanour of the person or those

I am talking with. I look for body language. If it's a phone conversation, I pause and listen. Most people just talk non-stop.

We babble about our ideas without watching the expression on our listener's face. You keep talking about that idea you had and that dream you have and how great it would be to get it done. While you are all excited about it, you should make it a point to watch the body language of the person you are talking to. Not everyone is interested as you are. Not everyone will support you; there are others who may even sometimes feel it is their personal ambition to stop you from ever getting anything done.So, don't just talk. When you talk, talk a little, pause, listen, watch and study people. Look for reactions; you will quickly learn those who are for you, with you, those who are against you and even those who are indifferent.

This is very important, don't just talk, observe, and listen to questions.Joseph told his brothers his first dream, he didn't pause to watch their behavior; he obviously didn't pay attention when their attitude towards him changed.

If he was watching, he wouldn't have told them the second dream.
First, he was being hated for being Daddy's favourite. Then

he had a dream and told his brothers, fueling the hate. Joseph didn't notice any of these hostilities because he wasn't paying attention. He was only interested in talking about his dreams.

"3. Now Israel (Jacob) loved Joseph more than all his children, because he was the son of his old age; and he made him a [distinctive] multicoloured tunic.

4. His brothers saw that their father loved Joseph more than all of his brothers; so they hated him and could not [find it within themselves to] speak to him on friendly terms.

5. Now Joseph dreamed a dream, and he told it to his brothers, and they hated him even more.

8. His brothers said to him, "Are you actually going to reign over us? Are you really going to rule and govern us as your subjects? So they hated him even more for [telling them about his dreams and for his [arrogant] words." - Genesis 37:3-5, 8.

Do you see what's going on here? Joseph's brothers were too angry with him they couldn't talk to him calmly. They would shout or reply harshly to him. Joseph didn't notice any of these hostilities; he went ahead and told them his dream. This made them hate him the more.

Don't be foolish. There are people who don't like you; there are people who always find a way to shoot down what you tell them, why do you still hang around? It can get you killed. Envy is real and not everyone has the mental strength to support people's ideas. Most of the time, we put ourselves in trouble by talking non-stop to people we don't have to be talking to at all.

Most of our problems in life begin when we become friends with people we should have just waved at and moved on.

That wasn't the end of Joseph ignoring the signs on the wall.

"9. But Joseph dreamed still another dream, and told it to his brothers [as well.] He said, "See here, I have again dreamed a dream, and lo, [this time I saw] eleven stars and the sun and the moon bowed down [in respect] to me!

10 . He told it to his father as well as to brothers.

11. Joseph's brothers were envious and jealous of him, but his father kept the words [of Joseph] in mind [wondering about their meaning]."- Genesis 37: 9-

Most of us behave like Joseph; the fact that you are excited about your idea doesn't mean everyone is excited about it. The fact that you are committed to your idea doesn't mean everyone is committed to it. I have behaved like that in the past. I have formed a team to work on an idea I had for a medical consultancy business. I thought everyone was as committed to the idea as I was. Reality set in when I realized it was my idea and not everyone was as enthusiastic as I was. I had to shut up and watch for reactions.

> "Not everyone will see the vision so don't
> bring everyone on the mission"

While Joseph's brothers envied him, his father pondered on his words. You see the sharp contrast in the reactions that followed?

28

While some won't support your ideas, there are others who will stand with you.

Lastly, in preserving our seeds, we need to avoid pests and insects. Your ideas will be attacked by pests and insects.

In this world we live in, all good would be attacked, all ideas would be tested. There are both internal and external factors that may affect your idea negatively. The major internal factors include fear, negative self-talk and self-doubt.

These factors may eat your idea away and stop you from ever embarking on making it happen. The external factors include negativity and other people's doubt. Don't let someone who never embarked on his journey talk you out of yours because of perceived perils.

This means you must jealously guard your idea from devourers, from negativity, from bad influence, from mediocre minds and people who are short sighted. Stay away from people who can't see beyond today, those who are only interested in temporary satisfaction. If you are looking to be among the reapers during the harvest and not regret in July, hold on to your seed, protect it and never allow anything to either rob you or destroy it.

This way, you will have plenty to eat in August. It's your idea, not theirs; protect it with all you have. Go after it as if your life depends on it because it does.

"A seed is useless unless it's planted. The most important seed in the world still has to be buried into the soil, away from everyone and everything before it can germinate into what it was meant to be. Plant your seeds."

CHAPTER TWO: SOWING THE SEED (IDEA)

"Sow your seed in morning and do not idle with your hands in the evening, for you do not know whether morning or evening planting will succeed, whether this or that, or whether both alike will be good." - Ecclesiastes 11:6 AMPLIFIED BIBLE

The popular saying, "you reap what you sow" has made people think reaping is an activity which follows immediately after sowing. Now more than ever, we need more patience as it's becoming a rare commodity in our generation. We want everything yesterday.

We want it instantaneously. With the advent of technology; it is even more evident in our daily lives how young people are losing the timeless art of patience. Jentezen Franklin put it this way: **"a microwave generation serving a God who cooks in a crockpot".**

We believe we can get everything in an instant, just like the microwave takes 5 seconds to warm our food. We have fast food and running stomachs. Martin Luther King Jr. described it as having "guided missiles and misguided men."

In this generation, we don't want to wait in line, we order stuff online, get them delivered in a matter of minutes to hours and often a few days. No one goes to the market to queue; we buy stuff online from our phones in an instant.

Technology is making everything easier, which is super exciting for me as a millennial.

My worry is that in a way we are transmitting this ease at which we live our lives into our pursuit of purpose. We believe we can reduce the time, create shortcut to success. For true success, time and hard work can never be taken out of the equation no matter how much technology we make available.

Just like Warren Buffet once opined, **"You can't get a baby in one month by impregnating nine women, some things just take time."**

This is what this book is talking about. We must learn patience and develop the tenacity to wait while we continue to invest effort and time into our dreams.

There is nothing like overnight success, you should know that already. Overnight success usually takes about ten to fifteen years.

I have seen young people become visibly frustrated after 5 seconds of waiting for a web page to load. I remember as a teenager, I was once at an internet café when a young man kept hitting the enter button on the keyboard repeatedly just because he has waited for 2 minutes for a video which hasn't loaded yet. I turned to him and said, almost shouting, "Can you just wait for it to load, can you just wait?"

We want faster internet. Fast network connections. I am not saying I would prefer a slow internet; not really, I am concerned that we think we can have faster success because we have faster internet.

We live in an era of urgent immediacy. There is no waiting anymore. Everyone wants it now.

Quickly, there is a difference between being patient and being lazy. I am not preaching laziness; I have already stated that. I am also not against technology, in fact, I love it. What I am saying is that, this generation needs to learn a little bit more about patience because we are losing it.

I have seen young people jump from one opportunity to the other, move from one company to the other simply because they are looking for a quick fix to success. We can't commit to anything because we are always on the move.

We can't hold down a job and simply gain experience before we move on to something else, we are always restless for something more. Nothing worthwhile happens suddenly. Great things take time.

Just like we have likened our idea to a seed, we should realize that it takes time to sow the seed, and sowing in itself is work. It was for me even as a ten (10) year old boy. It takes time to sow, it takes time for it to germinate, it takes time for it to mature and it takes time to harvest.

It wasn't easy for me as a ten (10) year old boy to sow three bags of maize on the farm. My job was to put three maize seeds in every dug hole on the land; cover it with dirt/soil. My elder brothers dug the hole, together with my mum, my sisters and I had the job of sowing the maize seeds.

It was child labour for me. I never enjoyed it, I sucked at it. I was often mischievous. I would plant extra seeds in order to run out of maize seeds, so I could rest.

What I did enjoy was seeing the seeds germinate and sprout into life but putting them into the soil wasn't something I looked forward to.

So, what I am driving at is, just as we have to sow our seeds, our ideas need to be sown as well. It has to be buried. Every idea has to be sown, hidden from the eyes of everyone, and buried in the soil, in darkness, until it's time to germinate. If you are looking to do something great, you should be willing to disappear for some time. Get off social media perhaps for some time so you can work on your idea.

As the youngest child, during the planting season, I helped as much as my ten little fingers would allow me.

Before the planting of seeds, there is waiting for rain. In Ghana and most part of Africa, there is greater dependency on natural rain as there are no or little artificial irrigation for most subsistence and small-scale farmers. When it doesn't rain, we are faced with a famine. Artificial irrigation was expensive and we didn't have the equipment. Not even water cans, and our farm was far away from the river where we could fetch water for our crops.

We expected rains and we almost always had it. When the rains delayed, we would walk long distance to fetch water from the river for the crops.

When we were sowing on the farm, the hardest part for me was obeying the rule of sowing two or three maize seeds per hole. You may think that's pretty easy but it isn't. After two hours of bending over, placing seeds in the hole, covering it with dirt, you would realize that you can't wait for your big bowl of maize seeds to run out so you can rest.

My elder brothers would get a stick, sharpen one edge of the stick; and that is what is used to make holes about 5cm into the ground. My only job was to count two or three maize seeds and put them in the hole, cover it up with soil. That's all I was supposed to do. I would obey the rule until my back started hurting, often, that didn't take long.

Don't call me lazy, I was 10; at this point, I would now put about 6 to 10 seeds in a hole. This approach was to help me finish my bowl of maize seeds faster. I am supposed to plant 2-3 seeds per hole; I now do it 4-6 seeds per hole. It meant I get to finish in half the time. You see, even at 10, I was really good at Mathematics :-).

There were days when I was really exhausted; I would pour fifteen (15) seeds into one hole. I would get away with it because no one has the time to double check how many maize seeds I was planting per hole. We often had a large piece of land to plant in a day and God knows how my mum had the money to purchase the maize seeds.

They were pretty expensive for her. She told me recently when I was writing this book, she had to store seeds from the previous harvest, borrow from friends and often bought the rest because she believed all the money she spent on the seeds would be recovered after the harvest.

My sins would be covered until the maize seeds germinated. For a few days, I would get away with it. When the seeds are inside the soil, no one knows what I did…yet.

34

After a few days, when we visit the farm to check on our planting work, you would hear my name being trumpeted. This meant they are seeing 10 maize plants germinating out of one hole. There was no need for a soothsayer to tell them who did that apart from their lazy last member of the family.

They would have to transplant some of the seedlings at other parts of the farm. That was not the end of my mischief on the farm. When it was time for us to weed after some weeks, I would end up cutting down some of the maize plants.

I was often too tired to weed out only the weeds so everything in the path of my cutlass or hoe had to go down. Also, I wasn't very much experienced weeding around the young maize plants without cutting down a few. The weeds are always found around the maize plants and required care in weeding them out.

It was fun and hard work on the farm. Sorry mum, I would make it up to you for all the maize plants I lazily cut down.

What I learnt on the farm contrary to the belief "when we sow, we reap" is that, when we sow, we don't reap immediately, we wait. Yes, we wait. There were days, I thought by looking closely at the maize plants I could see them growing.

I would stare at the growing young maize plants wishing they would start producing maize crops I could harvest instantly. This didn't happen, we waited, we weeded, we pruned, we fertilized sometimes, for weeks, months, and we would work hard on the farm. I often got frustrated.

My frustration was deepened often on my way to the farm. I

would see other people's farms with matured maize crops ready for harvest. I would get to our own farm only to be disappointed because it was only flowering or just about bearing crops.

I didn't realize each farm's maize matured differently based on several factors including the type of maize planted, the land conditions and the time of planting. These factors were never the same on each farm. So why was I fretting because someone who planted his or her maize a month or two months earlier had maize crops ready to harvest?

Just like how I felt when I was young, many people love to see other people's ideas sprout into life. We admire the results. We love success stories but we never want to plant our own ideas. We are not previewed to the efforts, the hard work, the commitment and sacrifice leading to what we see out there.

There are seasons, some are harvesting, and others are planting. If you are planting, work your field and don't be jealous of those harvesting. Your harvest will come.

We fret because we see the results of other people's work not taking into account factors such as how long the person has been working on his idea and the amount of effort and time invested thus far.

We don't want to go through the process, what we want is the result. It doesn't work that way. You don't have to focus on what you can see; ask what has gone into the building, the foundation.

Spend time on the foundation. You have to see the invisible to be able to do the impossible. See how much work there is and give yourself the permission to go through the process. Don't worry about the mistakes; we are supposed to make mistakes. Learn and grow.

You have to imagine your seed in the soil, your idea going through the dark days, finally sprouting and blossoming. Hold that in your mind and begin working on your ideas.

When the seed is placed into the soil and covered with dirt, it lies down alone in the dark, buried and out of sight. This is often a frustrating time, an enduring moment. We had to wait for days before germination.

Imagine my frustration at ten years old, going back to the farm the next day after sowing and the land was bare.

There was no sign that we have buried maize seeds into the soil. If someone had passed by, he wouldn't see the work we did yesterday. He or she wouldn't have the faintest idea what has gone into the earth.

It takes time for germination to occur and so it will for your ideas.

When you begin to work on your idea, people won't see it. Some may even laugh at you because they can't see what you see.

The energy, effort and money you invest won't germinate overnight. Friends and family will ask, "What are you even doing?" because they can't see what you are working on.

You may find yourself in darkness, withdrawn from the

society, you don't get to enjoy what others enjoy. Just like the seed in the soil doesn't get to enjoy sunlight, you may have to stay indoors for days, weeks and months just to work on your idea.

When someone asks me why I do wake up the time I wake up, I have one answer; "if you are going where I am going you will wake up the time I wake up."

You may have to stay up later than everyone else, you may have to skip going out; you may have to stop watching your favourite football club play, you may have to skip movies, less of social media.

This is the time a lot of seeds die in the soil. It takes fortitude to go through the dark period and to come out on top.

That is the time a lot of people get frustrated. Sowing your seed, putting your idea to work requires time and commitment.

It takes a lot of discipline to stay in the ground and go through the process. You have to be willing to hide yourself so you can work on your idea.

When I decided to write my first book, BECOMING YOUR DREAM, I spent long nights and early mornings writing. It was stressful, writing at night and going through my clinical internship program while working part time at a clinic 3 hours away from the hospital.

No one knew I was working on something like that, sleepless nights and tiring days of research. I knew I had to sow my idea and let it go through the process. I am in love with the process. After I am done with any of my books, I begin to miss the writing process. All I look forward to is writing another book.

INSIDE THE SOIL (DARK PERIOD)

When a seed is sown, it gets buried under a lot of dirt (soil). The seed is hidden from everyone and everything. This is a process many do not pay attention to, all we know is that it sprouts and blossoms. What happens when the seed gets buried deep into the soil? I will tell you.

For any idea to work, it must go through a period where it is hidden from everyone and everything. If you are looking to succeed, you must be willing to be hidden for some time.

You can't be everywhere all the time and still manage to dedicate time and energy to the project. When I needed to finish this book, I made the mistake of not giving myself any deadlines.

I had already published one book in March 2018 so I felt I could take my time. I have to finally commit before finishing it.

Again, I am writing about patience so why not be patient? I started drafting the outline for this book in October 2017 and I began researching in January 2018. I started writing in April 2018. It's February 2020, and I am just about finishing it up. I finally had to hide. I had to take some time off social media, no phone calls; I created time to work on finishing it by March 20th. It will require more of you than you can imagine, it will take longer than imagined so you have to be ready to endure when you begin working on your idea.

I went hiding for one month. Less of social media, more time devoted to writing. You have this book in your hand because, just like the seed, I had to sow it and let it be hidden from everyone. I was writing in the night.

It was lonely, I was itching to get back to active social media engagements but I knew what I was sacrificing for.

The dark period, the period when your life seems like you have been buried just like the seed, is a crucial one.

There are times in our lives where we may also feel like a seed which is buried. You may find yourself in a dark place and wonder what is going on.

When a seed is sown into the soil, it is covered with dirt; it's first out of sight. If you want to succeed, you must be willing to get out of sight for some time.

With social media, we are always online, telling everyone what we are doing, what projects we are working on, etc.

Great things always take time and this requires that you do take some time off the internet to work on your ideas.

This is different if you do your work online. The point I am making is you must be willing to be hidden from the public eye for a period of time if you are looking to achieve anything worthwhile.

You must be ready to be all alone in the room, working on

your craft. Nothing great was ever achieved suddenly.

For writers, being a good one is 10% talent and 90% not distracted by the internet. As I mentioned above, I decided to take a break off social media so I could concentrate and write this book. I took time off Facebook, Twitter and Instagram. I used whatsapp to stay in touch with my readers. I came back actively on Facebook to start gathering support for Beta Readers; this was also an idea I had to sow.

One thing you should realize is that you have to make the decision and back it with action. No one is going to ask you to turn off your Facebook, Twitter and Instagram accounts.

This is a decision you need to make yourself and back it with immediate action. I uninstalled the apps which were becoming difficult to stay away from. At the end of the break, I reinstalled them. I logged into Facebook using my browser. Typing in my email and password every time was too much work. That distracted me from easily signing into Facebook.

There is so much noise out there and in order for your idea to survive, you have to be willing to shut up, keep your head down and just work. Germination can only begin when the seed is buried in the soil. You cannot transform from where you are to the next level if you don't get buried.

If you don't hide and concentrate on working on your idea, you are going to remain as you are. Will you take a 30-day social media break challenge with me so you can work on your idea? I would like to support you. Send me an email. My email is in opening pages.

CHAPTER THREE: GERMINATION (THE PROCESS)

"Listen carefully: Unless a grain of wheat is buried in the ground, dead to the world, it is never any more than a grain of wheat. But if it is buried, it sprouts and reproduces itself many times over." -John 12:24 MSG

The seed contains embryonic parts, the cotyledon which when buried into the soil begins the germination process. It's now time for the seed to sprout into a seedling. The process of germination is an interesting one. I was always fascinated as to how the seed sprouts, gravitates towards light and water even in the soil.

Germination is the process of seeds developing into new plants. Seeds just don't grow; there are environmental factors necessary for a seed to germinate. Some of these factors leading to germination include how deep or shallow the seed is planted, the availability of water, and temperature. I have already mentioned in the beginning how important these factors are in ensuring the viability of the seed. Now, these same factors are more essential in ensuring whether the seed will germinate or otherwise.

Factors of Influence

It's important to note that several factors of influence affect how seeds germinate. There are quite a few factors to be considered but for the purpose of aligning them with how we can grow our ideas we will focus on water availability, sunlight and temperature. We would look at these factors and why they are important in ensuring our ideas also germinate.

There will be no germination without water. The seed first goes through a process called imbibition to activate the growth of the root. This is the process where the seed absorbs water into the cotyledon through the seed coat. Availability of water is therefore of prime importance in initiating the germination process.

Even as water is essential for germination to occur, too much of it will cause the seed to die. How does that happen? When a plant is still growing underground, during root formation, it doesn't have access to sunlight and cannot use the sun to make food like most matured plants do. The seed must therefore rely on the food in the cotyledon (stored food inside the seed) together with oxygen from the soil environment to produce energy. In a situation where the soil is too miry, there wouldn't be enough oxygen in the environment and the seed won't thrive. Imagine if you are kept under water with no way to breathe, how long will you last? That's what happens to the seed when there is too much water in the soil.

In growing our ideas, we already talked about sharing your idea with people who would help you develop it into something doable. So you will need water (support and experience from people who have knowledge to share) for your ideas to survive but expose it to too many people who will spit negativity on your idea and it will surely die. Just as a seed will die when exposed to too much water your idea would die when you go out there sharing it with too many people.

Just as the seed is to be exposed to the right amount of water, so should your idea be exposed to the right amount of people.

Another important factor in seed germination is temperature. Having the optimum temperature is essential for seed germination. There are, however, some seeds which germinate when they are in cold temperatures. These include plants in the northern environments. Some other seeds only germinate when the weather reaches spring temperatures, which is why we see so much plant growth in the spring in temperate climates. Other seeds only germinate after extreme temperatures, such as after a fire in the grasslands.

When we are preparing our farm lands for the planting season, we cut down trees to clear the land for planting the maize. Often, that land had been left to fallow for 3 seasons (3 years). Sometimes, we even weed out shrubs on an old farm, mostly left to fallow for a year for the new planting season. One common practice is to burn the weeds after weeding.

We believed that burning the weeds gets rid of all weeds and also make the land more fertile. Burning makes the land dark, rich and loamy. Later, I understood that the ash left over from burning adds potassium to the land.

There are some ideas which will grow even without a lot of heat, when it doesn't have a lot of people talking or working on it. You don't have to wait for everyone to get on board, sow it cold and it will germinate.

If you get an idea to start a YouTube channel on whatever you are passionate about, you don't need to talk to about it with 100 people before you start. Sow it cold, just go on YouTube and watch a few tutorials, begin with passion, just get some simple equipment and start. You will learn and grow a lot by just starting instead of looking to talk to everyone about it. I have also come to understand that clarity mostly comes from engagement. Stop waiting for approval, start.

About 18 months ago, I decided to start a Podcast talking about everything we need on the journey to becoming our dreams. I am building a legacy around my first book, BECOMING YOUR DREAM. I have a book and a podcast on it.

When I had this idea, I didn't know anything about podcasting apart from listening. I went on YouTube and after watching a dozen tutorials, I was ready. There are some ideas, the more you wait, the more you analyze, and the more paralyzed you become. It's called paralysis of analysis. So, some of your ideas don't need the heat of everyone, you have to sow it cold and generate the energy as you go forward.

Some seeds need extreme temperatures, some ideas require putting them through test after test, talking about it, subject it to heat and after it has withstood then it will grow.

You have to understand that it depends on the idea and the

kind of temperature required for growth. Take your time to study your idea; don't just start without due diligence. Even the ideas which require you start quickly will be successful only when you have a basic understanding of what you are getting into. A level of uncertainty is allowed, but being oblivious of what you are doing won't help you achieve. At least know what you want, the first step you need to take and learn on your way.

How Does Germination Occur?

1) The radicle pushes through the seed coat into the soil. The radicle later develops into the root of the plant. The plant first establishes its root. Without a firm root, you can't grow. Before the seed can germinate, it first anchors itself by growing the radicle.

These days, young people "shoot" up without properly anchoring their root. The shoot of the plant is what everyone sees outside the ground. Everyone wants to be seen right away. The most important aspect and in fact the first thing that happens during germination is the growth of the radicle. Just as the seed grows its root first, you need to do same. How deep is your root?

2) Primary roots begin to develop and the hypocotyl forms a hook that straightens out, pulling the cotyledons above ground.
The seed grows the primary root which holds the seed firmly

in the ground. After the growth of the primary root, it's now time for the shoot to go above ground. Stay with me, this is a process.

Like I stated earlier, the mistake of my generation is that we are rushing to grow our shoots when we haven't properly anchored our roots. I want you to get this principle into your mind and make it a part of your philosophy to concentrate on building strong foundations. Build the right foundations before building on your idea. If you get this concept, you can write this down in your journal, meditate on it. You can close the book and continue another time.

The hardest work is done on the foundation but no one sees it. The work that goes into the foundation of a building mostly goes unnoticed. We only ask about the foundation when the building is falling down or when something goes wrong with the structure.

If your life is falling apart, ask about the foundation of your life. If a nation is falling apart, look at the foundation. Anything without a strong foundation will come crumbling down.

Many young people have their lives falling apart because they failed to build strong foundations. If the foundation is right, you can erect your skyscraper without worrying about the storms that may come against it.

Matthew 7:24-27 MSG

"24. So everyone who hears these words of mine and acts on them, will be like a wise man [a far-sighted,

practical, and sensible man] who built his house on the rock.

25. And the rain fell, and the floods and torrents came, and the winds blew and slammed against that house; yet it did not fall, because it had been founded on the rock.

26. And everyone who bears these words of Mine and does not do them, will be like a foolish (stupid) man who built his house on the sand.

27. And the rain fell, and the floods and torrents came, and the winds blew and slammed against the house; and it fell –and great and complete was its fall."

Grow your root before you shoot up. Work on your foundations because the storms will come, the trials will come. If your foundation isn't strong enough then you will be exposed. If you are building a life, building a business, building your idea, you need to anchor your roots, build a strong foundation first.

When the maize sprouts out of the ground, it doesn't immediately begin to spread its leaves. Nature loves process and you cannot defy the natural order of events. Nature takes time, it may seem slow but nature delivers through a process.

3) The emergent seedling begins to straighten out, taking the cotyledons with it. Now is the time for the seedling to stand

up straight. At this stage of germination, the root is firmly in the soil and can withstand wind, rain, etc. coming against it.

If the seedling goes out of the ground too quickly, it will break against rain or wind. It won't be able to withstand the onslaught of the outside environment. Premature exposure has destroyed a lot of young people. We didn't properly develop our character before taking up certain positions, getting into certain relationships, building certain businesses, getting married, etc. We didn't know what to do when the bad times came to test our character. Again, build your foundation.

"Don't rush things that need time to grow; premature delivery can kill your baby".

4) The primary leaves begin unfolding and the stem elongates. At this stage, the leaves are now ready to spread and receive sunlight. Everything is a process.
Root first, leaves out next. Spread your leaves after and receive sunlight. This period begins the time to grow and mature. So remember this; first build a strong foundation and then go out there and show yourself. This is how you can survive out there.

The leaves at this stage are known as the primary leaves; these are not the true leaves. The true leaves are still protected inside the cotyledon. The more I understood the process of germination and growth, the more I understood how nature works. The plant doesn't go out there and quickly showcase all it has inside. There is a process for every dream or idea to work to its full potential. Without respect for the process, persistence and consistency, you are less likely to attain fulfillment. Many are rushing out there to achieve success, being swindled by get-rich-quick schemes because of their desire to attain success without going through the process.

"Committed and persistent work pays off; get-rich-quick schemes are ripoffs." - Proverbs 28: 20 The Message Bible

Go out there and do something small, measure the response, learn, ask questions and then expand. Growth should be a gradual learning process. Growth requires persistent action. The true leaves in the process of time completely emerge and the cotyledons eventually fall off. This is the end stage of germination. This is the time to fully unveil the true leaves. At this stage the seedling is ready to take centre stage. I love how nature works.

This process doesn't happen in a day. It takes days. Remember, we are juxtaposing the process of germination to growing our ideas. Your ideas have to go through these same processes. You can't jump steps.

What Factors Influence The Germination Process?

As stated, exposure to the right amount of temperature, good supply of water and how deep the seed is planted are the core factors essential to germination of the seed.

Often times, on the farm, everyone would be exhausted but we still had more bags of maize to sow. We would begin to act lazily; my elder brothers would start making shallow holes because they are too tired to dig deep.

Mum will begin rallying everyone not to get lazy for if we sowed into shallow holes then the rain would wash away the maize seedlings when they germinate. In addition, even if they survive the sweeping rain, they won't have firm roots to grow therefore limiting their yield. They would eventually fall down when the wind blows.

If you don't plant your maize deep enough, once it rains, your maize plant will be brought down by the moving waters. This is important for us as young people as well. Every idea we have, every dream we have or every vision we have should be planted deep enough. If we don't then when the hard times come and they will come, we would come crashing down.

There is a story in the Bible I will share here. Jesus shared lots of parables in the Bible and some of them are fascinating to me. This is one of them; let me tell you the parable.

Luke 8:4-8a

"4. As they went from town to town, a lot of people joined in and travelled along. He addressed them, using this story"

**5. A farmer went out to sow his seed. Some of it fell on the road; it was trampled down and the birds ate it.
6. Other seed fell in the gravel; it sprouted, but withered because it didn't have good roots.**

7. Other seed fell in the weeds; the weeds grew with it and strangled it.

8. Other seed fell in rich earth and produced a bumper crop. Are you listening to this? Really listening?"

This is such an interesting parable. You don't have to like it, you may not believe it, but there is something to be learnt from this on the subject of our conversation.

I just want to make sure you are getting this concept. When you continue to read, Jesus gave an explanation of what the parable meant.

For the purpose of our discussion; the type of soil you plant your seed in, how deep you plant will determine whether your seed will succeed or otherwise and subsequently your yield come August.

In addition to rain water in parenthesis for smoothness if you don't plant deep enough, your seedlings will also be exposed to the sun which cause them to wither. Remember Jesus' parable.

It is therefore important for us to not only plant in the right soil but also plant deep enough.

Don't sow in the gravel; don't sow at the shallow ground, dig deep and go deep.

Okay, enough of seeds, let's come out of the farm now and

look at how our ideas are doing.

Every idea should be well rooted in a well-resourced soil; a good plan and a strong force of action. It is not enough to move with just your instinct.

In the era in which we live, there are tons of information out there and the only way to succeed is to learn how you will marry your instinct with your intellect. Don't just feel but read, research, study, learn and then move forward with massive action.

Ask questions, talk to people who are ahead, learn from their mistakes, read the books, look at the reports. Go with your gut but listen with your mind first.

Don't let your mind override your instinct but most importantly don't let your gut override common sense. Don't be unwise. I have been stupid before in executing some of my ideas. I just go head in without due diligence. I learnt the hard way.

Now, the internet is my friend, Google is free to use (well, not really, you pay for the internet data and get advertised to by those who pay directly). YouTube has great tutorials. Don't ignore all of these and plough ahead blindly.

I won't begin unless I know most of what I need to know. I am saying don't be fooled into thinking you can achieve anything great by moving blindly by going with your gut feeling. Follow your heart but go with your brain.

What I have learnt is that, often times, blind optimism clouds judgment. Now, I am not talking about being 100% certain before doing anything; a level of uncertainty is necessary in the pursuit of our dreams.

What I am saying is, don't ignore the information available! Don't blatantly ignore the report. You don't have to follow it or do exactly as it says but read it. Know it, get the information. It's not so wrong not to know something but it's worse when you deliberately refuse to know. You don't have to like it, but you need to know it.

Listen to those who are saying it's impossible, listen to those who tried and failed, listen to them. I am not saying take their caution and stop, I am saying listen to them. I wish failures would give motivational speeches.

I have learnt a lot from people who shared their failures with me, more than from those who their successes with me. Pay attention to the "failure stories". Understand why they failed, why it didn't work, read the report, understand why they think your business idea won't succeed.

After you have done that, now it's your job to work around the obstacles, through them or over them. You are now fully aware of the possible challenges, you have been exposed to the carcasses of those who tried and failed. You are fully prepared to do whatever it takes to succeed at your idea.

Don't give up but before you plunge in take some time to understand what you are up against. Again, don't be stupid, get the information.

Like I said earlier, blind optimism sometimes clouds judgment. You have to separate positive idealism from reality while believing in your ideas.

Don't allow your self-belief and optimism to cloud your judgment about the enormity of the task ahead. Do your research, study the market, learn the trend and develop a plan of action.

Know how you are going to deal with the roadblocks. In this information era, develop the skill of skipping the noise and getting the substance of what you need. Don't let the obstacles stop you; let them fuel your passion to succeed.

That's how you sow your maize seeds deep enough. Without the proper background work done you are simply sowing into a shallow ground.

When the seed gets inside the soil, with plenty of water in the soil, the seed fills with water in a process called imbibition. There are special proteins called enzymes in the seed which are activated to begin the process of seed growth.

You remember the first thing the seed does during germination, right? The seed grows a root which goes deep to access underground water. It taps into the water around it.

You should also understand how important it is to tap deep into the resources around you when you begin working on your idea. I was working on one of my books; I reached out to someone in the industry who wasn't a friend. He was someone I only knew online.

I established contact with him, shared his work, commented in his posts, reviewed his articles and books. He helped review my book. He then wrote the foreword to the book.

I had to tap deep to make new connections to get what I wanted. I could have relied on what was around me, the same people around me but I needed something different.

What you started with, the water around you may not be enough to help you grow just like the seed. The information you started with may not be enough to help you grow your start up business.

This is the time to get connected to the right people. Dig deep for deeper waters. Learn what you don't know and be willing to keep asking "will you teach me how to do it?" Always, be ready to learn.

When the leaves are above ground, they begin to harness energy from the sun; the leaves will begin to grow towards the direction of the sun or the light source. This is a process called photomorphogenesis.

The plant knows exactly the direction it should grow towards to get what it needs. It grows towards the light, the right resource. Direction is more important than speed.

Knowing the right places to go, the right information to access, the right people to connect with to help you grow are essential. Read the right books, ask the right questions, and attend the right seminars and conferences. These things don't come to you, you find them.

You have to learn. You have to be mentored through the process.

CHAPTER FOUR: THE RAIN IS NOT ENOUGH, WE NEED IRRIGATION (MENTORSHIP)

"We all need some coaching because you can't figure it all out when you are in the game." - Jim Rohn

For some farming seasons, we couldn't get enough rain for farming. for all the years we farmed, I remember about three farming seasons when we experienced drought.

We would wait and pray (yeah, we prayed about everything) for rain. Sometimes, even with our best effort, our young plants wither due to the extreme weather temperatures. We prayed because we had no option. We prayed because we believe God can do anything. Our prayers were often answered, sometimes too it's like God is asking us to use our brains. I don't know.

We couldn't irrigate our farm using any other irrigation system; we only had rain as an option. We could dig bore holes but we didn't have the money or the man power (maybe they are excuses). Although, when I read the story of THE BOY WHO HARNESSED THE WIND..., I realized we could have done something.

In Ghana and most parts of Africa, we rely solely on natural rain to irrigate our crops and any change in rainfall pattern in a particular year would result in a famine. In 1983, Ghana suffered a year of severe famine because there wasn't enough rain in between 1982-83 for farmers to grow their crops.

In the last decades, we have adopted artificial irrigation methods which are still expensive for most of our farmers who mostly do subsistent farming. Many small- and large-scale farmers have now adopted reliable irrigation systems. Commercial farmers now have proper irrigation systems and don't rely solely on natural rain.

For us, we had an old stream not quite near our farm where we would fetch water with buckets to irrigate our crops when the rains delay. It was a lot of work to fetch bucketful after bucketful of water and walk a long distance to bring the water to our farm to water our plants. It was tedious but it was a task we couldn't skip because of the work we had already done.

We had sowed, weeded, and that was work enough we couldn't let go. Sometimes, the stream would dry out or not be enough because other farmers also relied on it. Just as nature sometimes doesn't provide enough rain for our crops, our ideas sometimes need artificial irrigation to survive. I liken irrigation of our crops to mentorship. No one ever does it alone. The rain was never enough most of the time.

"Without counsel purposes are disappointed: but with the multitude of counsellors they are established" (Proverbs 15:22 KJV).

WISDOM POINT: The only problem with your idea is that you are trying to do it alone.

Finding the right people who have travelled the path or know a thing or two about what you are about to embark on is like water to a withering seedling. It will save you a lot of trouble. Acknowledge when your plants need rain to grow.

Many would rather wither away than seek help. We don't ask for help because we are weak, we ask for help because we want to remain strong. As Jim Rohn opined; "We all need some coaching. It's hard to figure it all out when your head is in the game." I share this concept in my books because I don't only believe in it, I practice it and it works every single time.

You Can't Figure It All Out on Your Own

This is an important principle we need to imbibe on our journey to self-improvement. Having a mentor, someone whose advice you value and implement in your life is priceless. Listen to older people; you don't have to do everything they say but listen.

You should have people you listen to for their wisdom. This person could be a preacher, a businessman or woman, a friend, a parent, your teacher, etc.

Having someone who has travelled the path to advise you is an added advantage in developing your ideas. They would help you to avoid mistakes. Mentorship isn't only necessary but a key ingredient on the road to accomplishing our dreams.

I have several mentors and spiritual coaches. I have mentors for different aspect of my life and my spiritual coaches are for different purposes. There are mentors for business, for academics, for speaking, for writing, for relationships, etc.

Indeed, there are things that you do not understand how to do, but you don't have to worry your head. There is someone who has advanced knowledge to help you avoid all the mistakes and reduce the time you would need to succeed.

That is the essence of mentorship. Someone to point the way for you, he or she won't walk the path for you but would show you the way. As we go through life, there are things we will need others who have travelled the path to show us. You can't possibly think of everything, you can't possibly do it all alone, we could all use some help.

I love to tell a story of a boy in the Bible called Samuel. Samuel, before his birth was dedicated to God to become a prophet of God for the nation of Israel. There was an older prophet called Prophet Eli whom God was displeased with because of the disobedience of his children.

Samuel therefore was ordained to be Eli's heir. Even though Samuel was born purposely to succeed Prophet Eli, Samuel had no idea who God was and how He communicated with His prophets. He still needed to learn from the out of favour Prophet, Eli.

One night, as God called Samuel's name, Samuel thought it was Prophet Eli calling him and so he went to Eli. He couldn't recognize the voice of God. The only voice he knew was the human voice.

When Samuel got to Eli the second and third time as Samuel kept hearing the voice, Eli instinctively understood God was trying to speak to Samuel. Eli was old and an experienced prophet. Eli said to Samuel on the third time, "if you hear the voice again, respond to the voice saying, "Speak, Lord, thy servant listeneth." (read the encounter in I Samuel 3:2-15)

Samuel did and God finally spoke to him. Samuel was only able to recognize and respond to God after Prophet Eli showed him the way. So, sometimes, regardless of what we think we know or how destined we think we are for greatness, it is important to learn from people who have travelled the path before us.

There is no self-made man. Everyone who ever did something great had help from others. A mentor, either for personal development or spiritual, will ensure that you understand how to prioritize your time and go after the things which matter.

You should not just go about it without knowing what needs to be done first. There are people who spend too much time doing things that they do not even have to do. There is nothing worse than succeeding on the wrong goal.
In the end, you'll realize that you've left out the things that matter most. However, if you have a mentor, you can be sure that there will be no need to worry about such things as they will be well taken care of. All that is needed from your part is to ensure you heed the advice of your mentor.

Allow yourself to be irrigated so you don't wither waiting for natural rain. You can't figure it all out, stop wasting your time. Being patient doesn't mean trying hopelessly to figure it all out yourself.

CHAPTER FIVE: GET THE WEEDS OUT

"I don't know the formula for success but I know the equation will not add up without hard work." - Rudolph Mensah

Weeds will grow without any invitation. Problems will show up without you calling them. You have to deal with troubles which come up uninvited. Weeds will grow whether you want them to grow or otherwise.

I always wondered how weeds came about on our farm. We would clear the land, burn the weeds, sow our maize but after about three weeks, here come the weeds. No one invited them, we didn't plant them, and they just sprang up.

That's life, things happen, you may not have invited the problem but you have to solve it.

On the other hand, if you want to grow orchids or hibiscus flowers at your backyard, you would have to cultivate them. They won't just grow. Our maize didn't just grow, we had to plant it. The weeds just came up without invitation.

That's life. Problems, challenges and disappointments will show up mostly without our invitation and we have to weed them away. But the good things you desire in life have to be cultivated. They won't just grow.

We sowed maize but when they germinated, weeds came with them. We have to weed them out or they will compete with the maize plants for nutrients. This would deprive the maize plants of the required amount of nutrient to flourish.

In addition, a weedy maize farm would be a safe habour for rats, grass cutters and mice to come in and devour our plants.

So, weeding our farm was non-negotiable.

I never enjoyed weeding as a child. Weeding was not funny, especially when the farm tools available were hoes and cutlasses. Weeding could last between a week and a month depending on the farm size and the work force available.

We could weed till our palms were red and the skin peeling off. We hardly had money to hire additional farm hands.

I cried, I cursed and vowed to never let my kids weed on the farm. At age 12, I still detested weeding. There were days when we had to weed on pineapple farm, which was much harder work. Pineapple has small spikes which scrape your skin. We often had to dress up in trousers and long sleeve shirts with gloves to be able to weed on the pineapple farm. I won't talk about that for now. Let's get back to the maize farm.

There was this old woman who had her farm on the way to our farm. We had to pass her farm before getting to ours.

This woman, although old, was worn out physically and couldn't even stand straight, yet was on her farm almost every day I went by her farm. We would always find her on the farm. She had a small chair on the farm. She would sit on it and weed around her farm moving the chair as she advanced.

As at the time I was 12, she was 91. When my mum told me her age, I just couldn't believe a 91-year-old woman would be strong enough to work on the farm. She went home carrying cassava and maize from her farm, sometimes we would help her carry her foodstuff.

Whenever I found myself on our farm fuming about how tired and hungry, I was, I would begin to think about this old woman who was still working hard.

She embarrassed me by how hard she worked at 91. She was one of the reasons why I don't like being around lazy people. I resolved to be a hard worker too.

"He becometh poor that dealeth with a slack hand: but the hand of the diligent maketh rich." - Proverbs 10:4 KJV

On working on your ideas, hard work can never be taken out of the equation. Work is a principle, God instituted right from the beginning.

God blesses your hard work. You can't be blessed when you are lazy. God doesn't bless lazy people. You can't be idle and expect God to bless you. In fact, God hates laziness. The first instruction that was ever given to man was to work. How can God then ask us not to work? Hard work won't kill you.

"And every plant of the field before it was in the earth,

and every herb of the field before it grew: for the **LORD God** had not caused it to rain upon the earth, and there was not a man to till the ground. And the **LORD God** took the man, and put him into the Garden of Eden to dress it and keep it" **(Genesis 2:5, 15).**

Man's first assignment on earth was to work. Work wasn't a punishment. I have heard a lot of people say God punished man to work after the disobedience. That is far from the truth, we realize from Genesis chapter 2 that long before the disobedience, man was mandated to till the ground.

Whatever you find yourself doing, give it your all. Laziness isn't a sign of wisdom. Wise people don't get to work late and leave early. Wise people don't laze about at work and expect to be blessed.

They work. They are dedicated to hard work. They don't sleep for hours and wait for blessings. They burn the midnight oil and give it their all. Their trust isn't in their work but in God who blesses the crops of their labour.

Work and you will be satisfied with plenty so you can give to others. Be a blessing. Wisdom works. "Some people don't deserve rest, rest is for people who work, and some people are always tired from doing nothing."

Part of the process of developing patience on the way to our dreams is the understanding that hard work is essential and we can't run away from it.

On the farm, I understood that we had to work hard, weed out the weeds or else we would lose our maize plants to rodents and restrict the plants from flourishing. Continuous learning is the minimum requirement for success. The moment you become complacent, that's when the weeds grow.

Keep working hard on your ideas and don't let the weeds take over. Keep weeding out everything which will choke your idea. In order for your idea to keep blossoming, you need to keep out the weeds.

Keep out the negative people, keep out the pessimists, and keep out any negative behaviour that might be hindering the growth of your ideas.

You don't get out the weeds by going to the farm and repeating, "there is no weed, there is no weed, there is no weed."

No, I am not preaching that. I am not an affirmation man; you can only affirm what you are willing to follow up with action. We get the weeds out by pulling them out.

If you are facing a challenge, take action, do something instead of thinking and wishing. Action is the foundation for all success as Pablo Picasso once opined. We don't solve our problems and challenges by reciting affirmations.

On the farm, we weeded. We pulled out anything which wasn't good for the growth of our maize. The ultimate goal here is to nurture your maize to grow to their full capacity in order to give you a good yield.

CHAPTER SIX: SOMETIMES YOUR BEST IS NOT ENOUGH

"Do your best until you know better and when you do, do better."- Maya Angelou?

Sometimes just having an idea and taking action won't be enough to get you the result. Working hard on your idea may not be enough. Watering it isn't enough, talking to people isn't enough.

You have done all we have discussed in this book; you gave it your best shot but what do you do when your best is not enough? On the journey to becoming your dream, working hard, committing to excellence and putting in every effort may sadly not be enough to reach the top.

That's the truth. Sometimes you do all that is required but still come short.

There are times in our lives where even though we are on the right path, we seem to never get to our destination or achieve any level of success.

Someone once said, "even if you are on the right path you will get trampled over if you stay there too long."

We never liked the idea of using fertilizers on our farm for two reasons; first, it was expensive and secondly, we would rather mulch. Mulching is a traditional form of agriculture where dead leaves or plants are used to cover a soil space in order to increase the soil nutrients.

It reduces the absorption of heat by the soil; and the decay of the plant materials covering the soil adds nutrients to the soil, etc.

So, instead of applying fertilizers, we would mulch. This was a natural process and takes time. However, there were some farming seasons when we needed to apply fertilizers on our farm, especially the vegetable farms.

We would not get a good yield if we didn't. So, together with mulching, we would have to do everything to afford fertilizers.

One day, on the way to the farm, one man's farm had a stretch of green maize plants while ours were growing yellowish leaves. I was curious; inquisitively I inquired from the man why his farm is so green, was it because he planted different species of the maize or a different brand?

We had "local maize" and "hybrid maize" which we called "agric maize" growing up. Many farmers had started using the "agric maize" but we couldn't afford so we mostly used the "local maize."

The local maize took six months to mature while the "agric maize" took half that time. This meant we had to work and wait for long to harvest our maize.

Our advantage was that the local maize could be stored for a longer period and still retain their nutrients. This means we get to keep our maize over long periods of time, sell them on the market and eventually have some seeds to plant during the next planting season.

When I asked the man why his farm had such a stretch of green maize plants, he told me he applied fertilizer to his farm.

My mum as usual made a way where there seemed to be no way. I never understood how she took care of us with nothing. We were also able to apply fertilizer to our plants. In a week or two we started to notice the difference between applying fertilizers and not applying them.

Our plants also started turning green to our delight. We added our traditional mulching and that further enhanced their growth.

We had done everything right but we were still short of what we expected. If we were going to harvest healthy crops, we needed to apply the fertilizer.

In developing our ideas, we need to do the same with them. We have to do what we can and when that is not enough we have to do what is required.

Every idea will require some evaluation and adjustment on the way. How you started it will not work out all the way. You may start out selling paper towels but by the third month it's imperative to change your business model or delivery plans.

You will need to inject fresh perspectives and add new methods of executing the idea successfully.

Do the best you can with your idea but if that's not enough to get you the required results, it's time for you to do what is required. Apply fertilizer.

During the growth of the plant, the available natural conditions may not be favourable enough to ensure it yields the desired harvest.

For several seasons, there wouldn't be enough rain, not enough sunshine. Depending on the soil conditions, there may not be enough soil nutrients.

At this stage, there is the need to take a step back and look at what's needed to make our crops grow to fruition. Now, there is the need to add fertilizer to the soil to enhance plant growth.

Ask yourself; what will I do when it doesn't rain? What will you do when rats invade the farm? What will you do when army worms invade your farm? What will you do when the soil nutrient isn't enough?

Don't just plunge into action until you have considered all possible challenges and how you will surmount them. There is no way you will ever be able to know every challenge you would have to face but you can anticipate many of them.

Other people have shared their experiences, read books, ask questions and know how to navigate the quagmires.

Most importantly, ask yourself questions. What will I do if I run out of money, what will I do if I don't get clients to pay for my service or product, can I do without an office space? If my online store is hacked, do I have security protocol in place to make sure clients are safe and my data is secure?

You have to be prepared for how you will deal with all these challenges because they will come. It is not a straightforward process from sowing to reaping.

There are obstacles on the way and you need to be prepared.

If your idea needs an injection of new perspectives, then do it and don't hold on to your initial idea.

Mark Zuckerberg started Facebook with his team to connect students on Harvard campus, look where they are now. When you recognize the need to apply "fertilizer" so your idea doesn't die, do it. Most people become stubborn at this stage and lose all their hard work.

Don't keep to your old ways when you are experiencing stunted growth. We had many farmers who never believed in fertilizers and they always had a small yield. If you have to apply fertilizer, then do it.

Do all you can and if that is not enough then do what is required. If you start selling a product and the market isn't appreciating it, it's time to take a step back and evaluate the product. Why don't they like it?

Can I get some people using similar products to give me honest feedback on why they won't use mine?

Can you make it better? What can you add to it? Is it something people actually need? Can I modify it to meet their requirement? Am I selling to the right segment of the market?

I had to ask myself, for instance; what can I add to this book to make it better? If you had read the first draft of this book, you would have rated it a negative 1. I started by telling my story on the farm and I realized I was talking about memorable childhood moments I enjoyed. With emphasis on "I", it however didn't make meaning to someone reading, what values are there to be picked up by the reader. My childhood has memories I cherish but how does that help you the reader?

When I asked myself this question, I decided to spend time to research and talk about my time on the farm juxtaposing it with how we grow our ideas. So, now, even though you are reading about my time on the farm as a 10-year-old, you are also getting some values on how to develop your ideas and be patient with the process of becoming your dream.

In the process of growing your ideas, and life itself, take some time to ask yourself questions on what kind of impact you are looking to make. If your product isn't selling, consider the sales approach. Would it be beneficial to take a sales course from an expert? Do it, fertilize your idea. Don't allow your idea to die. We are surrounded by information and you must learn to tap into the right channels to help you make your ideas work.

PRUNING

What is pruning? Pruning is an agricultural process where we cut away [often dead] parts of a plant in order to allow the healthy parts to grow well. Pruning allows proper absorption of sunlight and increases aeration around the plant. When dead parts are cut off, it stops often the infected parts from spreading to the healthy parts.

In developing your ideas, there will be the need to cut away the dead aspects of the idea and allow the thriving ones to grow well. You must understand when to prune in order to grow.

Many tend to hold on to everything and lose it all in the end. You need to learn how to cut away certain portions of your plan in order to have a workable plan. When I wrote my first book, it was 400 pages. After my mentor had gone through and my editor has done his job, it came down to 300 pages. I was asked to read through and accept or reject the changes made. I had a hard time accepting that certain aspects should be taken out of the book. I held on to some pages I never wanted to let go.

Finally, I had to agree to take away several other paragraphs till the book came down to less than 250 pages. This happened with my subsequent works as I always found it difficult "pruning" some ideas out.

As I am writing this book, I have come to understand more why there is the need to prune. There were lots of ideas and concept I wanted to include in this book but I pruned them out.

In order to grow, you have to be comfortable with getting rid of the things which do not help you advance on your purpose. Often, we have to cut away healthy parts of the plants in order to allow the remaining parts to get nutrient and increase the yield. We had to sacrifice some plants to allow the rest to grow.

I often come up with multiple ideas which all sound good and intriguing to pursue but in order to be effective, I have to keep some of them away [for a time] while concentrating on the ones I can work on.

You have to be comfortable with shutting some doors of opportunity in order to concentrate and work on just one. Don't spread yourself so thin, concentrate your energy on a specific goal.

"When a man's undivided attention is centered on the one object, his mind will constantly be suggesting improvements of value, which would escape him if his brain was occupied by a dozen different subjects at once. Many a fortune has slipped through a man's fingers because he was engaging in too many occupations at a time. There is good sense in the old caution against having too many irons in the fire at once." --- Og Mandino; University of Success.

When you do all you can and it's not enough, do what is required. Do your best until you know better and when you do, do better. You can always do more and life will require more of you.

CHAPTER SEVEN: PATIENCE, WHO HAS TIME FOR THAT?

"Success isn't instant noodles. It doesn't take three minutes to cook. You can't microwave success. It doesn't take three seconds." - Rudolph Mensah

This is an era of urgent and immediate gratification. Patience, who has time for that? Who has time to wait in line to buy something from the stores? Who has time to wait for three months for a shipment of arrive? It's irritating to wait in line for hours at the bus stop or airport just to get on a bus or an airplane. Waiting isn't funny. It's fatiguing to wait. We sit down at the restaurant and after five seconds if the person waiting at the table doesn't rush to us, we flag him or her down. Often, we do that angrily.

Technology has allowed us to earn a university degree online in 6 months, could be less or more. Soon, we won't have to pack our bags and go to college anymore. Right behind the computer, with the aid of a stable internet connection, we can study in our pajamas from the comfort of our rooms from finest universities around the world.

In ten years, who really will have time to go to college for four years? Soon, traditional universities will be more online than on campus. Colleges will still operate but 50% of it will be online. People will stay on campuses, live in dormitories or residential halls but will have most of their classes online. They will download lecture notes on a dedicated website with exclusive student's access; live stream lectures, etc. I can see us getting there.

This will relieve pressure on public university facilities especially in developing countries. This is a bold prediction and I wouldn't be far from right.

We order products online and we get them delivered to our doorsteps. Distance is no longer a barrier. The world is now more than ever a global village and as Bill Gates once said, "the internet is the town square".

We watch movies on demand, when we want it and how we want it. In the past, (I haven't been here for long, less than three decades but I can tell you how much things have changed) things were not like that. Growing up, between the age of 8 and 14, we had to wait for programs to come up on Television. We had only one accessible and popular TV channel in Ghana, the Ghana Television, GTV. There were other private televisions coming up but the only channel almost every Ghanaian had access to was GTV.

You could wait all day for a program to come up and the television station can decide to cancel the program. We were at the mercy of the national TV channel as to what we get to see. These days we demand what we want, how we want it and when we want it. Children born today won't understand what that means, to wait for a program to come up on TV.

We didn't have a remote because there were no alternative channels to change to. There was no choice.

In the past, people had to walk long distances to deliver messages. Then we had horsemen and messengers on chariots who delivered messages. The advent of postal services was an industrial revolution. We still had to wait several months or weeks before our letters get to their destination.

Sometimes, you are not even certain of the letter getting to the destined person. You can only hope and pray. Then, it was such a revolution when we were able to speak on the telephone using wires.

There were skepticisms about the telephone. One person, Sir William Preece, Chief Engineer, British Post Office, in 1878, had condemned the idea of telephones, "The Americans have need of the telephone, but we do not. We have plenty of messenger boys".

These days we have text messages, so we can send messages in seconds. Interestingly, we even send money over the phone now. We speak to people long distances apart through the air. We don't need wires anymore. We have wireless devices.

With each technological advancement; we have reduced time spent on waiting and increased efficiency of getting things done. Inasmuch as this has revolutionized our world, it has robbed this generation of learning the skill of patience.

I am not writing this book as a 72-year-old man who is perplexed about the pace of technology. I am writing this book as a 27-year-old young man who is well accustomed to the technology of our time, a millennial who lives his daily life with technology. I often wonder how it feels for my mum who is 60. She has expressed her disinterest in using a smart phone. She prefers a phone with keypad. She had to go through some training to understand how to use the simple handset so she wants to stick with it. She could learn but she just doesn't care enough to put in the effort. She is comfortable.

Am I then implying I am not happy about all these technological advancements? Of course not! Life would be tedious and boring if we were still walking long distances to deliver information.

What I am saying is; the older generation understood what it meant to wait. To be patient and trust that things happen with time. Patience was a skill well ingrained in their system. You were forced to wait for things to happen and that taught them patience. Our generation has been robbed of the opportunity to learn the timeless skill of patience. Technology has virtually removed and reduced waiting. As wonderful as this is, it has also denied us of the opportunity of learning how to wait and be patient in life.

With the push of a button, we get things done and so we translate this same attitude to life we tend to think everything must happen with the push of a button.

These days, no one has time to wait. If a company doesn't find the technology to reduce the waiting time, customers are leaving them. Everyone is looking for faster network, internet which loads faster. Every telecommunication company is looking to provide faster internet service. The same with the banks, everyone complains of how long they have to wait so banks are bringing banking online. It's all about reducing waiting and increasing speed of service.

We live in an era of how fast I can do something and still be effective. Let's talk about that for a couple of minutes because we miss the point entirely. It is not about how fast you can do it but how well you can do it correctly no matter how slow. Efficiency and speed are two different entities. It doesn't however mean they can't occur together. I am not saying you have to be slow to be efficient; my point is, if you have to choose between speed and efficiency, choose efficiency no matter the speed.

The only way to work with speed, reduce mistakes and still be efficient is when you develop a strategy. Developing a strategy requires patience, commitment and dedication to deep work. You need time to gain mastery over your craft which will then help you to develop strategy. Strategy then allows you to work faster and still be efficient.

So, I am not saying it's not possible to be fast and efficient, I am saying it requires patience. That is what most people still miss in our generation. We are just speeding nowhere fast. If you don't know where you are going then running faster won't get you there.

Now, when we get ideas, what do we do? We jump right into it. As much as I agree you have to take action quickly on your ideas, you first need a plan to execute. Without a plan, you are setting yourself up for failure.

Spend time to plan but move on to execution and then review your plan, modify and continue executing.

Execution is important to achieve anything worthwhile. So, for every idea we get, we must act on. Think slowly about it but act quickly. The thinking should result in developing a plan. You don't need to be 100% certain or fully understand how everything is going to work out, you just have to begin. Clarity comes from engagement. As you work, you will begin to understand and learn more about the idea and how you can make it better. Again, clarity comes from engagement.

Then again, speed is an essential element when it comes to putting our ideas to work. Ideas love speed. The longer you wait, the more likely you will abandon the idea and not work on it. Speed here doesn't cancel patience; however, you can't lag around; someone else may run with the idea. If you want to operate on the global scale then it's important you understand that speed contributes to success. More significantly, remember direction is more important than speed.

Let's bring it altogether now; what am I driving at with this talk about speed, efficiency and patience?

My point is; speed isn't a bad thing and that we shouldn't laze around in the name of being patient. We shouldn't be slow when we can be fast just because we have to be patient. I want you to however ask yourself the question; where am I going?

Answer that first and we can talk about how long it will take you to get there. The speed or duration is of no importance when we haven't established the destination. When we have established the destination then we need to understand that it won't happen overnight. That is when being patient with the process becomes important. When you sow, you don't reap immediately.

So, when you know where you are going, start working on it right away. Believe in the process and be patient knowing that we shall win, maybe not immediately but definitely. As you continue to work and develop mastery, you will learn to develop strategies which will help you move with speed while still being efficient.

This is what a lot of young people have trouble with. When we sow today, we want to reap tomorrow. Like my friend Peter Kwadwo Asare Nyarko says; "the day you sow the seed isn't the day you eat the fruit."

Let me take you back to my farm, my mum's farm actually, our farm, anyway. Often, when the maize plants start growing, they first grow green leaves and keep growing more leaves until they start producing flowers.

When it starts flowering, it's an indication that we are nearing the crop bearing stage.

This process of growing leaves and bearing flowers doesn't happen in a day. It takes weeks. Even though we had planted, watered, weeded, pruned and weeded again, we still had to wait.

There was no chemical to speed that up; there were no magical incantations to make it happen in minutes, there was absolutely nothing we could do except wait for the plant to go through the natural process. Nature respects process, it doesn't rush.

I read about a **study conducted at the University of Arizona** in 2009 where over 30,000 emergency call centres in India were analyzed.

Out of the calls terminated within 2 minutes after being put on hold, 52% of them reported they hang up to find another way to solve their problems or to redial again.

Ask yourself; why after just two minutes, someone who was calling for emergency service can't wait to get assistance? Patience, who has time for that?

Again, data from Velaro showed that all it takes is waiting on hold for one minute and almost 60% of customers will hang up. In their study, nearly more 2,500 consumers were surveyed. Almost 60% of the respondents believed that 1 minute is too long a time to hold on, 32.3% of the respondents said the customer service departments should be answering their calls "immediately" – no need to hold on. About a third of the respondents when asked what time would be ideal to hold answered; no time, they are not willing to wait at all. 27.6% answered 1 minute and 4.1% affirmed they would as long as it took.

In another study at the University of Massachuset, Associate Professor Ramesh Sitaraman and collaborators at Akamai conducted the first large-scale study of its kind to quantitatively demonstrate how video stream quality causes changes in viewer behavior. 6.7 million internet users were surveyed. The amount of time users waited for a video to load was 2 seconds. After 5 seconds, a quarter of them had abandoned the video and after 10 seconds half of them were gone.

Some people visibly become angry because they had to wait for a video to load. Impatience leads to anger. The truth we should all come to terms with is that 'we can't speed everything up".

"The crop of patience is always sweet." - Pakistan Proverb

Everything is a process and not everything is under our control. We can't press some keys or push a button to get everything done. It takes patience to build a worthwhile idea into fruition and experience true happiness.

Our generation is getting used to pressing buttons and keys to get things done. We bring this same attitude to life and feel we can push buttons and become great overnight. We can become famous overnight on social media but greatness requires time.

Let me take you to a typical classroom. Slow readers are suppressed; the fast readers take over every reading activity. The intelligent students determine the speed of reading. They dictate the pace because they are allowed to read while the slow readers are considered a nuisance as they slow down the reading in class. No one has time to wait for the slow readers and learners to catch up. We push them out, they are asked to follow the fast readers or be left behind, the latter is often the case.

We need to encourage the slow readers to keep reading. Not how fast they read but how correctly and well they can read regardless of the speed.

Let's go to a restaurant, what do we see? Right after we sit down, we immediately flag down the waiter or waitress. When the person waiting the table doesn't come to us in a minute, we are already losing our patience.

Do this; the next time you go to a restaurant or a place to eat, take a seat, sit down and don't flag the waiter down. Relax; allow some time to pass, let the waiter come to you. Unless of course you are starving to death which is never the case. Spending ten minutes waiting won't make any difference. Calm yourself and don't be in a hurry. If you had planned your evening ahead, you wouldn't be rushing out.

The more we are forced to wait the more we can learn to be patient. Put yourself into situations where you are forced to wait and, in those instances, you will learn to be patient.

Everyone wants it yesterday. Gary Vee says "speed without patience leads to mistakes. The essence of strategy is needed to act fast and still be patient."

For every idea you are working on, start small, and start now. Begin by building the right foundation with patience, establish yourself locally and think on a global scale. As you learn and build, you gain experience, you get to know what works and what doesn't, you develop strategy, soon you can be fast and efficient.

Waiting is one of the hardest things you will ever do in your life if you are looking for long term satisfaction. You will never be truly successful if you are not patient. Again, patience is not lazing about. Waiting doesn't mean lying around the beach doing nothing; waiting is putting in the work and trusting the process. Understanding that it won't happen overnight.

You can't always look for shortcuts to success. Every shortcut will cut you short in life. There is no elevator to get you up there; you have to take the stairs.

Great things take time; you have to be patient; you have to work hard. Stay faithful and improve on your craft. Wait and you will surely win.

Don't become a casualty of haste. Everything is working for you if you are working for everything. It may not be immediately, but definitely.

We are not running out of time, no, we are rather running so fast that time can't keep up with us. However, direction is more important than speed. It's therefore more important to know where you are going.

Know what you want, start working on it, teach yourself to understand that it won't happen overnight, it will happen overtime. Enjoy the process, have time for patience.

CHAPTER EIGHT: JUST A LITTLE WHILE

"Some things just take time; you can't get a baby in one month by impregnating nine women." - Warren Buffet.

After weeks of working on the farm, we begin to see results. The maize began to bear crops. You may think that's good news but this was a tempting period. When you have been waiting for far too long for something, how you behave when you are close will determine what happens to it.

Often, you feel like something is close yet not yet in your hands, too close yet seems far away. This is a test of your endurance, this is a test of your staying power, can you wait a little longer? Can you hold on, it's almost here but can you wait just a little while?

Especially for me as a 12-year-old boy, immediately the maize started bearing crops, I was tempted to proceed to harvesting. My mum and elder siblings somehow understood waiting at that point better than I did.

On arriving at the farm, I couldn't sit still until I plucked and roasted the maize crop only to find out they aren't matured.

Mum would give us a stern warning: "they are not matured yet, don't pluck them, we have waited for weeks so let's wait for one or two more weeks, you won't die."

We won't die, yes, but sometimes waiting felt like dying. This is how waiting feels for most of us, to wait when it seems all others are ahead of you.

Mostly, I would disobey. I didn't do quite well following instructions on the farm. Seeing the maize crops fresh on the maize plant, I think to myself; they are matured. I would pluck one, remove the husk and roast it. Sometimes, we throw the maize with the husk on into the fire. It was fun eating maize on the farm.

After removing the husk, I would realize the maize isn't fully matured.

There was nothing to chew. I would then have wasted weeks of work because I couldn't wait for a week or two for the maize crop to mature. I have had this same experience in different aspects of my life. I have seen this happen to many people, who after working so hard for something ruined it at the last minute because they couldn't wait just a little while.

Often, because we have suffered or waited far too long for something, we don't have the patience to allow it to work to full fruition. We sacrifice long term fulfillment for temporal satisfaction. Never be in a hurry to celebrate because of what you have suffered through the process.

It's tempting to show others you are also succeeding. What I have learned is that you don't want to be exposed too quickly. Give time some time.

Always look for long term fulfillment so you don't grow up with regrets. Many will give up just at the one-yard line. You have invested money and time into your idea; you start making some profit and you begin spending.

Can you exercise a little more patience and reinvest your money? Can you give yourself five years without luxuries and expensive phones? Can we wait some more? This stage on the farm was more daunting than the weeks of sowing, weeding, mulching, and irrigation.

As I dedicated myself to personal development and living a life of service to others, I have always known I am on the path to personal fulfillment but I am not there yet.

I have waited, I am still waiting, I may be close but it's still not yet in my hands. Can we still wait some more? Can we trust the process a little bit more with the faith that we will get what we seek? Waiting requires more strength than most people can bear but it's an important part of life.

What makes it harder? We have to pass other farms to our farm. We will get to our farm hungry, looking at other people's matured crops, sometimes with a tinge of envy. I never understood the emotional turmoil and how hard that was, writing about it is bringing me all the emotions. It was hard, really tough.

This is it; this is where life will test your resolve. When you sow you don't reap immediately. You wait, you wait and you wait some more. Are you getting tired? Hold on. We have to wait some more. What do you do when you have waited, you are already tired of waiting and then you have to wait some more?

Most people will act like I did when I was young; I would settle for immature maize crops then regret my actions later. Don't be like most people. Trust the process. **You didn't come this far just to come this far. Wait.**

I will end up destroying three months of working, waiting, weeding just because I couldn't wait for one or two more weeks. That's it, two more weeks and then the maize crops would mature.

You will get to a stage of your life when you are so close to success yet so far away. You have done everything right, you have invested time and effort, you have committed every resource to this project or idea but still you have nothing to show for it.

This is not the time to fret, continue to believe in the process as you have done since the beginning. Don't waste all the time you have waited, keep the faith and believe in your dream. You are already in pain, get a reward for it. You are already hungry, wait a little.

As my mentor says, "stay on the path". You are doing a lot of things; you have done many things right but this is the time for you to keep the faith and keep going.

Remember the words; we shall win, maybe not immediately but definitely.

CHAPTER NINE: LET'S REAP

"Those who sow in tears shall reap with joyful singing." - Psalm 126:5 AMP

It's a joy to harvest; all the months of hard work and struggle are in pale comparison to the joy of harvesting. We went to the farm hungry, we sowed in pain and distress but now, all of that are in the rear-view mirror. Reaping brings joy to our hearts and smiles to our faces. We don't remember how hard it was during the day of weeding, irrigation, pruning, waiting, fending off rodents, we are simply focused on the harvest.

Our maize crops are finally matured, we schedule a time to reap. We wait too long; rats and grass cutters will devour our months of work. We wait too long and it rains again, it will destroy our months of work. So, you see, even after the crops are matured, timing and work is needed to get the harvest done well.

We have to decide on the quantity of harvest to be stored, the quantity to be sold, quantity to be eaten, exactly when and to where we will be transporting them to.

How much we are going to save for the next planting season, how much we are going sell and how many sacks we are going to keep in our kitchen to prepare our staple foods. We make all these decisions with reaping.

Reaping is work. From sowing to reaping is all work. Everything is work. Listen; there is no way around hard work. If you are looking for anything without hard work, you might want to buy lottery tickets, good luck with that.

You have to get to work, don't look at the weather.

Make no excuses.

"He who watches the wind [waiting for all conditions to be perfect] will not sow [seed], and he who looks at the clouds will not reap [a harvest]" - Ecclesiastes 11:4 AMP.

If you have worked your idea to this point, then you are ready to harvest. Don't let anything distract you. There were days when we had to harvest in the rain because if we left the maize on the farm for the rains to fall then the maize will start germinating on the cobs. It will spoil. So, the weather wasn't an obstacle, regardless of the weather, we harvested.

Reaping is done with a plan. A plan for how we will be harvesting and a plan for how we will be storing and preparing for the next season. The crucial decisions you have to make when reaping is; where will you be storing, how much will you be saving, eating or spending, investing or saving for the next season?

You need to come with a plan for your money, your time, your resources, etc. We never started reaping until we knew exactly what we will be doing with the harvest. Sometimes, we were faced with bad weather (rains) and we had to get everything out of the farm but then quickly come up with a plan on what to do with it.

Decide how you are going to invest or spend the profit or gains from the idea you are working on. Without a plan, when you get the money in your hand, you will end up spending it on "unnecessary" things. Just because you suffered for your harvest doesn't mean you are at liberty to spend as you please.

Always have a plan for what you will do when your idea takes off. What will you do when you have a breakthrough? What will you do when you hit an obstacle? When working on an idea, you should make projections and write down possible solutions and plans for what you will do.

Thinking about all these gives you the opportunity to think through and be thoroughly prepared for what's ahead.

Don't go harvesting without a plan for what you will be doing with your harvest.

How much is for spending? How much is for investing? How much is for charity?

Don't eat your seed.

CHAPTER TEN: STOREHOUSE IS FOR THE INCREASE OF CORN

"Storehouses also for the increase of corn, and wine, and oil;" - 2 Chronicles 32: 8a.

In the past, agriculture was a crucial part of society for survival. It formed the foundation for society. During winter for instance, having food in store determined whether you and your family survived or started to death.

The Biblical verse above is talking about the agricultural principle of storage which can be equivalent to saving at the bank. Like we discussed in the last chapter, before reaping we had to decide how much maize seeds we had to store for food or for planting the following farming season.

However, this generation has been taught to buy without money. We buy with credit cards; we buy on hire purchase and we are falling into the trap of instant gratification. Many financial institutions find ways of getting young people to spend on expensive gadgets forcing them to run into debt. We are made to think that we can buy now and pay later. Regardless of the interests and inflation, we simply buy.

We are instantly gratified so we spend everything we have, and then some more and even what we don't have yet. We can get almost anything on credit. There is no need to wait for anything anymore. There is no need to save. I am passionate about what I am sharing because I have been at both ends. I have experienced how spending without a plan can hold you down and how big a mistake it is to spend everything you get.

According to the verse above, **"we can only increase our corn when we keep them at our storehouses."**

When we store what we harvest, we accumulate and have enough to invest, grow again and give to others. In the epilogue of this book I talk about "don't eat your seeds".

We should learn to store what we harvest if we are looking to increase our corn. We can only build true wealth if we can delay instant gratification for long term satisfaction.

"First plant your fields; then build your barn." – Proverbs 24:27 MSG

This Biblical verse above is an agricultural advice from King Solomon of ancient Israel. What has this got to do with us today?

This advice comes from the agriculturally based society of Solomon's time. During that time, people's survival depended on the state, readiness and yield of their fields. In other words, the size of your farm and the quantity of your farm produce determined not only your chances of survival but livelihood.

If a family had little or no yield of crops, the family runs into famine and that is not good for survival. Therefore, the highest priority for everyone at the time was to keep their field in good condition and have food available for the family.

I have told those close to me I won't buy a car until I have parcels of land and a plan to build my house. I should have a representation of a house or build my house. This may seem to you like a bad idea but I believe that having priorities in life is a criterion for success. This is my priority. It doesn't mean that if you have need for a car, don't buy a car. But remember that a car is going to take money away from you (fuel and servicing) and if it is not bringing in any income, why buy it? You should get a car to work to bring you money, not only for convenience.

As a young man beginning life, Solomon is advising us to "get our fields ready" first, what does that mean? This means, first, get a job or begin one which will put food on your table, most importantly, keep food on your table. This is very crucial for your survival. When you don't have what to eat and consistent source of basic life needs such as food, you are likely to run into trouble, advised Solomon. Get work first, have something to eat and postpone pleasure.

After that, "build your house", Solomon says. This is a great summary of priorities for a successful life. Work, get food on the table and build your house.

To bring it into our contemporary world, this advice would be, "make sure you are ready to make a living, have a place you call your own before you start to enjoy life's pleasures."

You have to put in the work needed to begin your career, get and keep a well-paying job or start your own business.

After you have gained the skills to provide for yourself and your family, you should then take time to build your house and begin thinking about building your family.

Getting a good education is a requirement in our era in order to prepare your fields to make a living. I was fascinated with my study of this verse and as I expounded more on it, I came to a conclusion that this is the best advice every young man or woman should heed to.

First, have a career, get and keep a job, be able to provide for yourself and your family, you can start your own business if you want to; build your house before you begin to indulge yourself in the pleasures of life. Always remember this; work before pleasure.

If you don't heed to this advice, soon winter will ask you what you were doing all summer. If we will survive the coming winter and be alive till the next planting season, we needed to know how we will store our harvest and plan for the coming year.

Storehouses are for the increase of corn. If you don't want to struggle for corn during the next season, then you need storehouses to store the corn.

This storage isn't only to have food for next season or planting but also that is how you increase. That is how you build wealth. That is how you increase your success. Many people talk about what they used to do, who they used to be, because they did something in the past and didn't know how to increase it. They lost it along the way.

If you are looking to increase in any area of your life, you should learn to have storehouses for keeping your corn.

> **"There is a treasure to be desired and oil in the dwelling of the wise; but a foolish man spendeth it up" -- Proverbs**

This is also a distinction between the wise and the foolish. Foolish people like to spend everything according to the book of proverbs. I have been foolish and now I am wise. How you use your harvest is therefore an indication of whether you are wise or foolish. Wisdom builds with the future in mind, the foolish only thinks about today.

Inasmuch as we are thinking of building a lasting legacy and achieving what we set out to, we should be concerned about preparing for the future.

Are you going to spend everything you just earned through hard work, commitment and patience just because you suffered to earn it or you are going to develop the mental fortitude to delay temporal gratification for long term satisfaction?

EPILOGUE: DON'T EAT YOUR SEEDS

I was going to write another book just on this chapter for two reasons; it's a subject on its own and two, I wanted to spare this book a few more pages. Nevertheless, I might one day write on this subject alone into a separate book.

Many of us when we attain a level of success, when we reap our harvest because of the hunger we have endured so far whet our appetites and we feel we owe ourselves a treat. We will buy ourselves everything money can buy, why? Because we have suffered.

This mentality will always bring you to square one. You are never going to reach your highest potential if you have to always satisfy your whims.

In the last chapter, we talked about storing or keeping your harvest for the future but don't kid yourself because you put money in the bank you have the discipline to keep it there. In an era where we are attached to motivation, a study says there are about 2 billion views on the subject of motivation on YouTube every day.

People like to get motivated but don't want to do anything. So, after reading this book you decide to keep some money, delay buying that new car or spending on that vacation but it takes more than deciding, it takes action. I can only inspire you, challenge you but real motivation comes from within.

You should find reasons within yourself to hold on, to keep spending at bay. To stop yourself from moving when you should stay, to stay on the job and learn, gather experience when you have spent two years already but everyone is moving and you feel like you need to move as well.

Sometimes all we have to do is to hold on and not sacrifice everything we have done so far.

Your seeds are the crops of your labour. You have earned the right to enjoy it, to eat to your fill but it is also expedient that you think long term and delay eating everything today. Don't forget about tomorrow, it's just around the corner.

I have tried to draw the line between forgetting to live today and being so much future focused and having a balance between enjoying your life today with the future in mind. You should therefore understand that I don't mean denying yourself everything today because of tomorrow, you need to find a balance.

The verse in the book of proverbs says "the foolish spendeth it all". You have to keep some of your seed for the next planting season. Don't eat it all. Ants think summer all winter and think winter all summer. Always looking ahead to the coming days.

That is an exhibition of wisdom. I have had a peculiar attachment to this book because I have witnessed so many people losing their lives, marriage, relationships, ideas, future because they were not patient enough.

Because they were in a hurry to get to the destination, they missed the trip and fell. Imagine if you are going to a place and have to pass through the countryside, you are speeding at 150kmph and so you miss the scene, you miss taking time to smell the flowers, see the real countryside, even though you got to your destination, you missed the whole point of the trip.

The journey is the destination, the process is the result. Have the destination in mind but enjoy the process.

You have your seed in your hands now but what you do with it will determine where you will be during the next planting season.

Will you be wise or will you be foolish?

Until I see you again in my next book or my next post on my website or social media platforms, don't eat your seeds.

If you have been patient enough to read through the whole book, I would like you to read the last few pages, don't go yet. A little more patience, you may find one sentence in the last few pages that may give you the idea you need to succeed and that is all you may need.

Don't run off in a hurry, if you have learnt anything in this book, it is to wait to see everything to the end and to go through the process and not be in a hurry.

PLEASE LEAVE A REVIEW

Did you like WHEN YOU SOW YOU DON'T REAP?

Before you go, I would like to say "thank you" for purchasing this book. You could have picked from dozens of books but you took a chance to check out this one.

So, a big thank you for ordering this book and reading all the way to the end. Now I'd like to ask for a favor.

Could you please take a minute or two and leave a review for this book on Amazon?

This feedback will help me to continue to write the kind of books that help you to take action and get results. Will you help me?

Please visit my Amazon author page:
www.amazon.com/author/rudolphmensah.

OTHER BOOKS BY RUDOLPH MENSAH

Available on Amazon.

Becoming Your Dream

Leap

31 Days of Wisdom

365 Days of Inspiration

Set and Achieve Smarter Goals

ABOUT THE AUTHOR

A young dynamic speaker and lover of God, Rudolph is devoted to helping people find meaning in their lives and become what they dream of. His first book, BECOMING YOUR DREAM, has been a first-time sensation globally.

He is also the author of the books 31 DAYS OF WISDOM, LEAP: ACTION; THE BRIDGE BETWEEN KNOWING AND DOING, SET AND ACHIEVE SMARTER GOALS EVERY TIME and 365 DAYS OF INSPIRATION.

He continues to share insight on his website and social media platforms with thousands and speaks to several hundreds of audiences. Rudolph is also a doctor; a job which brings him closer every day to patients' struggles and pain. When medicine can't heal them, he touches them with the special balm of the love of God and a super sense of motivation.

His philosophy in life is that, "life has no meaning until you define it and when you define your life purpose and you put in the work, then you shall win, it may not be immediately but definitely."

He is a native of Elmina in Ghana and continues to work to improve the health of rural communities in Ghana.

www.ingramcontent.com/pod-product-compliance
Lightning Source LLC
Chambersburg PA
CBHW021445210526
45463CB00002B/636

* 9 7 9 8 6 7 6 0 6 4 4 8 8 *